BOBBI LEE
Indian Rebel

By

Lee Maracle

Foreword by Jeannette Armstrong

women's
P R E S S

CANADIAN CATALOGUING IN PUBLICATION DATA
Maracle, Lee, 1950—
    Bobbi Lee, Indian Rebel

New ed.
ISBN 0-88961-148-3

1. Maracle, Lee, 1950 —   . 2. Métis — Social conditions.*
3. Indianism Treatment of — Canada. 4. Métis — Women
— Biography.* 5. Métis — Biography.*

FC109.1.M37 A3 1990   305'.897'071   C90-094555-9
E99.M69M37 1990

Cover art and design: Shirley Bear
Editing: Viola Thomas
Copy editing and proofreading: Midnight Sun

Published by Women's Press, 180 Bloor St. W. #1202
Toronto, Ontario, Canada M5S 2V6.

This book was produced by the collective effort of Women's Press.

Women's Press gratefully acknowledges financial support from
The Canada Council and the Ontario Arts Council.

Printed and bound in Canada.
    4 5 6 7 2005 2004 2003 2002 2001

Oka Peace Camp — September 9, 1990

The tension is thick, heavy with the reality that here on the eastern end of the country there have been 400 years — 400 years of colonial battering. The pain of the relatives is palpable. My sympathy, my sense of support changes to stubborn ancient rage. The air changes. Terry D. looks at the women, speaking softly, poetically, trying to persuade them to return to camp.

It is cold, especially as night draws near. The summer has receded. It has threatened to freeze and the women know these people cannot stay behind the razor wire much longer. It is comfortable in the crowd, one of the anonymous faces for a change. The minutes tick by and with every second the police have time to organize themselves. No one seems to be concerned about the growing numbers of Sureté du Québec amassing at the farmyard just one block away. We wait while the women argue for marching into the arms of the police. It strikes me that most of the people standing around came here to do just that — march down the road to the Treatment Centre. I look out across the street to the park. The Sureté du Québec are busy. Their ring gets tighter. This is too much for some of the supporters. Cars begin pulling out. Some white guy is shouting to come back and is confronted by a woman who is fed up with a white man shouting at us. The crowd is split in half now.

We can't possibly get through the S.Q. lines. Terry tries to reason with the women. It isn't news. We all know to march would be disaster. Many people will be hurt, possibly killed. "Don't tell us we haven't been hurt," and I start thinking of my dead brother, my dead brother-in-law, aunts, uncles, cousins, friends, most young, some childless. And I find myself preparing for death, preparing to leave my children motherless because it feels like maybe bloodletting is what this country needs. Maybe if we just let the road to Oka run red with the blood of women, someone in this country will see the death and destruction this country has wrought on us.

Quite calmly and almost absurdly my memory rolls back to a conversation with Daphne Marlatt who said, "Gee, you seem to go to an awful lot of funerals..." I remember the hot rage in my throat being pushed back by a cool disposition. "Yeah, well all those statistics have relatives and friends you know, some of them mine." Softly I pour water on the fire in my throat. "Yeah," Daphne says, and I can't help wondering if Canadians can truly see us. See that we truly do love one another. We know the Mohawks are not anyone's saviour. We know they are all folks like ourselves, but after centuries of the colonial state pressing on our villages, taking life after life, we are finally fed up.

Some Métis leader from the Northwest Territories spoke against the Mohawks. I remember what he said: "They are drunks and criminals." I read that and wanted to call him on the phone and ask him if he thought our lives so cheap that he wanted us to be killed for drunkenness, and what sort of crimes did he think we had to commit to be shot? Clifford Olson comes to mind. A serial killer, white, male, alive and well in protective custody, charged with the murder of a large number of innocent children. I wonder why this Métis leader thinks we ought to be killed for merely being accused of drunkenness and criminality by white officialdom.

I think about what has happened to us in the last sixty days. In every major city, on the reserves of 37 First Nations homelands, people rose up to support the Mohawks. We are beginning to like ourselves, and unlike the Métis leader of the Dene territories, we feel we have a right to live. Churches, labour organizations, women's groups, all kinds of Canadians objected to the army being brought down on Oka.

We want peace. Peace, freedom from warring conditions, freedom from conditions which annoy the mind. Violence, an unjust and unwarranted attack, to distort meaning and understanding.

This country is a battered country. The land is scarred with extraction in the interest of corporate imperialism. The language is battered: battered in the interest of sanctioning the scarring of the land in the interest of profit. Strip-mining, uranium production, gas and oil extraction, mega hydro projects, clearcutting, over-fishing, chemical disfiguring of the soil, tampering with foodstuffs are all carried out in the interest of profit. All are referred to as progress and development. Potato chips and processed cheese, that is what advanced civilization amounts to. We know development means to nurture, to grow, and extraction for profit is not nurturing and neither are potato chips and processed cheese.

For us language is sacred. Words represent the accumulated knowledge, the progression of thought of any people. To distort meaning, understanding, in the interest of pacifying a whole population in the face of massive rape and exploitation, is the worst kind of violence. This country knows in its heart we have never been violent. We have never in our history distorted meaning or attacked anyone unjustly.

Creation is sacred. We are obligated to retreat into the deepest and most complete thought and work out the direction of our life based on our personal sense of solidarity with all creation before making any decisions. Even when we defend ourselves we do so peacefully. Our love for earth, for human life, prohibits us from attacking earth and life. What is different today, is that we know it is just to defend ourselves. We know we are worthy of defense. Unlike the Métis leader of the Northwest Territories, we feel, we believe, we think, we have a right to life.

Creation is not passive. The birth, re-birth process of the earth, her storms, eruptions, tidal waves, floods, droughts and the coming of periodic ice ages attest to a total lack of passivity. The birth process of the plant and animal kingdom is not passive. Individually, every living thing on earth must labour to re-create itself. Seeds burst from the shell to regenerate and the process of birth for mammals is accomplished only with much blood shed.

The re-birth of any social order is not passive. We cannot live in this world the way it is. What is it when the mayor of a foreign town can come into your backyard and propose to play golf on the graves of your dead? What is it when that foreign country forms its own internal laws to make this despicable act legal? At no time in history have Europeans ever suggested playing golf on their own graves. Yet gravesite after gravesite of our dead are considered accessible for the most ridiculous of pasttimes.

The train of rape and defilement stops here. When we stand up to say enough, every single Canadian benefits. The laws which guide us, the love of life, our life, which moves us does not stop at our doorstep. The racist structure of this society only thinly veils the class structure. The reality of this country is that many Canadians are having a hard time, financially. Poverty lurks in the living rooms of two million citizens. The homeless are increasing geometrically in urban centres and they are predominantly white. The cycle of recessions which began in this country in 1973 has led to a spiralling down of the standard of living of the citizens of this nation. The state is more than aware that to satisfy the demand of a single Native reserve is to have to satisfy the demands of all of us. The state is also aware that to meet our demands for a decent life would mean upgrading the lives of thousands upon thousands of single white Canadian mothers, and thousands upon thousands of working poor.

Peace. There is no peace in this country. We are absolutely opposed to a bunch of cowboys in a D-9 cat running hi-diddle-diddle over the hill playing Texas chainsaw massacre with our trees. Peace: freedom from conditions which annoy the mind. It annoys our minds to sleep under the dome of imperialist lust which is constantly looking for newer and more effective means of attacking our homelands, clawing and digging at them, extracting the insides, covering our graves with roadways, golf grounds, housing projects, offices, or what-have-you.

We are absolutely opposed to anyone, organized with machine guns, assault rifles and tanks invading another people's territory to play shootemup cowboy. It takes great effort on our part not to leave the barricades and run all over the town of Oka playing shootemup cowboy. Despite the abuse, the cheapening of our lives and our homelands, we don't do it. We still believe life is sacred.

Peaceful struggle is all about expending great, strenuous effort to live free from strife, free from war, free from conditions which annoy the mind. It annoys our minds to imagine golfers tramping on the grave of Mohawk grandmothers. It annoys our minds to think, to feel, that we are less than sovereign people in our homelands. And it annoys a good many Canadians now too.

This summer, if anything, the state convinced a good

many Canadian white people that it does not give a shit about any of us. These opinions mean nothing when it comes to us. Money is the only speech the state is prepared to hear. We don't have any money and Canadians in general have less and less each day. Mulroney and Co. heard not a word from the thousands upon thousands of us who walked, marched, blocked roads, picketed, bought ads in newspapers, wrote, spoke on television and telephoned.

The state is aware that should our laws prevail anywhere in this country, the heyday of corporate imperialism is over. The difference is that now we care enough about our sacred being to get up and say no, and the echo of that no continues across the country.

If we are all dead we cannot have peace. If we are allowed to die this country will be left with their violence. They will be left with the memory of inactivity in the face of our genocide. Many of the citizens of this country are not prepared to accept the violence of the state against our people any longer. They know we have done all the unjust dying a people should have to do.

More than that. Apathy is a kind of admission of insignificance, a form of self-erasure. Some of the citizens of this land wish to be significant. They refuse to be erased. They want peace and solidarity, with each other, with all people and with the earth. And they are prepared to actively search out this peace, be resolute and caring about the promise of solidarity.

We/they are refusing to be obedient. From July 11th onward we will listen to one instruction only — love our own. We have been busy over the past summer deciding who "our own" are. They are a range of colours: black, red, brown, yellow and white. And we can recognize them by their loyalty to justice, peace and solidarity. Oka, the people of Kanesatake, brought that home to us.

We did not shed our blood on the streets of Oka. No surrender was negotiated. The men and women tried to make a run for it. We all know that we must talk. Really talk — from a position of wholeness, completeness — about building a sustainable movement in the country that will lead all of us to justice and peace. We know that the country is capable of sending in the troops. This is not Vietnam — we cannot call the boys home if they are in our backyard.

The life of Bobbi Lee is about why we must talk.

LEE MARACLE

BOBBI LEE
Indian Rebel

Foreword

The documentation, together with the telling of the Native sojourn through the quagmire of Canada's colonialist past is an extremely important human document to Canadian literature.

In particular the telling of our lives, the back-tracking, the map-making through the treacherous terrain of our individual experiences is perhaps a more important exercise than we Native people readily appreciate.

Lee Maracle's book, written in the 1970s is one such contribution. This book is spoken at a time when writing was not considered a "useful" endeavour in the on-going struggle of our peoples. I speak of struggle to uncurl from the somnambulistic fetal ball, survival state that psychological oppression had reduced our peoples to, in the aftermath of the totalitarianistic measures to dispossess our peoples of everything that is meaningful in life.

This book spoken and then edited into written form, is reflective of the wonderful orality that the spoken version must have been delivered in. In the movement of the life story of Bobbi Lee, what unfolds is the story of many natives during those times. There were real conditions which shaped the people like Lee. The harsh realities of the day, seen through the mix of native and non-native values and customs jammed together for survival purposes is a clear portrayal of the chaos created from the external into our various lives. Yet the clear path toward transformation through personal resolve, resistance and clear thinking is a path that Bobbi sharpens into focus, strong as the formative ideals that burgeon into a strong native political and cultural renaissance immediately following the period the book covers.

JEANNETTE ARMSTRONG

Dedication

At 2:00 p.m., Friday April 25, 1975, Don Barnett, chairman of the Liberation Support Movement, comrade of the Native Study Group and leading proletarian socialist practitioner in North America died. The blow to me was tremendous. I was stricken by the news and, at first, unable to deal with it. The aspect of life which idealist philosophy can least rationalize is death. Having come from the soil of bourgeois society, I found traces of idealism lingering within me. Its expression was my inability to deal with this, our first death. Idealists deal with death by shrouding it in mystery, burying the body while reifying the "soul." For Marxists there can be no comfort in such nonsense.

Is then a man's life to come into being and pass away uselessly, as though he never was born? Indeed in North America many are born and die in just such a way, leaving nothing behind but the fallacy of long hoped for "eternal life." Not a single mark on history do they make and so they just die. For deaths such as these there is little for loved ones to do but grieve their loss and hope for the hopeless — life after death. For a man to die without ever having made any contribution to his fellow human beings, to pass out of being without having participated in the great forward march of human history, there is much to mourn. Such a man dies and is soon forgotten.

Don was not such a man; to mourn his death would be to deny a lifetime of constant participation in struggle and the great contribution he made to the development of proletarian socialism. For those of us who knew him, were guided, criticized and inspired by him, there can be no mourning. It is not that we do not feel his great loss. His loss weighs heavily upon us. The setback that his death means to the struggle for proletarian socialism here in North America is a real one. He was a young man who had only greater contributions to make. Nor is it that he died unloved. We all loved him deeply. Our love must not be wasted in sorrow but rather must manifest itself in our willingness to take up the struggle for proletarian socialism with the same determination and unwavering tenacity that so characterized Don. It was this determination to struggle at a time when winning seemed impossible, against odds that seemed unsurmountable, that inspired us and reshaped our lives. To mourn would be to anchor ourselves to a past which Don had cast aside and led others to do the same.

It is in this spirit that I dedicate both volumes of my life history to Don.

Prologue

There are two voices in the pages of this book, mine and Donald Barnett's. As-told-tos between whites and Natives rarely work, when they do, it's wonderful, when they don't it's a disaster for the Native. Don never intended it to be a disaster for me. The first *Bobbi Lee* was the reduction of some two hundred pages of manuscript to a little book. What began as a class to learn how to do other people's life history, turned into a project to do my own. We had disagreements over what to include and what to exclude, disagreements over wording, voice. In the end, the voice that reached the paper was Don's, the information alone was mine.

At the time, I did not know enough to do it myself, nor argue him out of the way in which my life was presented. I wanted to re-write the whole thing. But it didn't seem fair to the memory of the original book and the readers who loved it. Further, I was a very distorted child at the time of the first book. I didn't like white people. Period. I respected Don, at times almost liked him, but not quite. I didn't, couldn't tell him everything. There were too many obstacles in my path.

He did inspire me to get command of my voice. He believed I had great potential, but was quite raw. He also tried to groom me to 'lead' people to political struggle. But his idea of political struggle was riddled with arrogance, something I loathed, but knew I too was full of. I jumped ship before I got too caught up in his style of organization with its centralist leadership. I have not figured out what kind of organization we need to pull us out of the mess we are in, but I know the existing forms don't work. In leaving,

I decided to seek out that 'lonely attic' in which writing, theory, story and life is imagined and put on paper.

It took a great deal more than a pen and paper and my unabridged dictionary. But in the end, all my ambiguity about white people and my loathing for them died. I have come to love his family since his death. They have suffered tremendously. They have struggled to put their lives together without the arrogance, the sexism and the racism they had inherited from their society and had not under Don's 'leadership' rid themselves of.

The Barnett children, save Lori who perished, are loving human beings. Daphne Gray is now blossoming into the wonderful woman she always wanted to be, but couldn't. Independence, self-reliance and writing are now a part of her. I remember Don once said his wife was 'almost an intellectual.' It scared me then into silence. Now I see it as so much white male narcissism that kept him arrogantly rooted in autocratic behaviour. In the absence of Don, I have grown to love Daphne, formerly Carol Barnett, and her children. Love is not always a many splendered thing. We don't see each other enough, or write to each other enough, but the loneliness from missing someone you love is better than never having loved at all.

Turbulent Childhood

I was born in Vancouver on July 2nd 1950 and raised on the North Shore mud flats about two miles east of Second Narrows Bridge. My first memory is of something that happened when I was about two years old. My brother Roger and I were playing down on the flats, catching wee little crabs and putting them in a quart-sized jar — which seemed huge to us because we were so small. Suddenly, I knocked over the jar and all the crabs went scurrying away. Roger yelled "Babe!" — they all called me "Babe" then — "Go and get them!" Well, I ran behind a log where they had headed and got stuck in some deep mud. Roger was scared. He thought I was in real trouble and bolted up the trail from the beach to get mom and dad. Dad came down, picked me up out of the mud and patted me; he was so strong it seemed he was spanking me and I wondered why.

My mother, born in a large Métis community in Lac Labiche, Alberta, is the child of a Frenchman and an Indian woman. She grew up on a farm and at nineteen travelled to Edmonton, where she found work as a domestic for a rich Jewish family. Father was born on a small farm in Goodsoil, Saskatchewan, and grew up during the drought and depression of the '30s. People had a hard time then just staying alive, especially those who depended solely on their crops. In addition to the bad times, my grandfather was old and had arthritis, so it was very difficult for him to tend the farm.

As a young boy, my dad trapped animals to support the family. At fifteen he was out on his own, hopping boxcars, travelling around trying to find work. At twenty he joined the army and was sent to train in Edmonton, where he met my mother. Then he was transferred to Jericho, Vancouver. He wrote my mom many letters and finally he asked her to come to the coast and marry him. He was 22 and she was a year younger. They hadn't really known each other very well, mainly through letters, and it wasn't long before they started fighting and getting on badly.

Three years after they were married they had a son, Nelson, but he died at eleven months. A second son, Ed, was born when mom was 27 and he's still alive. In two-and-a-half years there was Roger, and I came along eleven months later. My two sisters, Joan and Joyce were twins; they were born on 12 June 1952. Gordon was born in May 1954, and George in November 1959.

The house we lived in had originally been an RCMP boatshed; my dad nailed hardboard sections (rooms) into the top part where we lived and worked on building and repairing boats in the shed below it. There was no electricity — no heating, hot water or other luxuries like television. We didn't get electricity till 1953, but even then the place was always cold and damp.

Until I was three I spent most of my time with my dad's father. Then later, when dad was around more, he would paddle us out in his rowboat to shoot ducks, which we learned to do quite young. I remember the first time clearly. I was standing in the skiff aiming intently at some ducks, but when I pulled the trigger it was too much for me — the jolt knocked me back right into the water. Dad grabbed at his gun and when I popped out of the water he was angry at me for almost getting it wet.

Later, dad started fishing off the docks in Steveston, which was about twenty miles from home. I helped the other kids gut the fish he caught. Sometimes mom left the babies at home with granddad and came along with my two older brothers to help.

When I was three years old I still didn't talk. My parents were worried about it and took me to see a doctor — several, in fact. I found out later they were psychiatrists. My folks were always arguing about me. I was often left with a woman named Eileen Dunster — whom I called "Aunt Eileen" — because dad kept beating me up and mom didn't like it.

Though I didn't talk, I remember watching things and thinking a lot. I don't know why, but I was a very serious kid. Once mom came in and said "It's raining cats 'n' dogs outside!" I ran to the window to see, but was disappointed to find only the usual rain drops coming down. I wondered for a long time why she had lied like that.

My silence lasted another year. Then one day mom caught me talking to Roger, with whom I was very close, and after that the jig was up. I started talking a little with my parents, but not very much; I didn't like big people. I thought they were interesting, but not people I wanted to talk to.

My parents fought a lot — nearly all the time. When they had parties — which was almost every week — dad got drunk and made us kids drink beer too. He would then make us dance and do other stupid things — which I really hated. I remember the first time I thought I hated my dad. My sister and I had this game: we would both run into the house and the first to touch the toilet seat got to use the bathroom first. Once my sister pushed me away from the toilet seat when I clearly had her beat. In retaliation I pulled her off the toilet and she peed on the floor. She was crying and told dad. He ran in and slapped me hard in the face. I didn't cry; I just stared coldly at him. He then turned and left the house. I was four years old.

Around that time things got really bad in the family. The old man was always beating up on Ed, my oldest brother. He'd throw him against the wall and sometimes end up hurting him pretty badly. Dad started being gone a lot of the time, but when he came home we would all run away. Ed started staying away for days. Once, when he was 13 and I was 9, he was gone for almost a week. Mom got real worried and kicked dad out of the house, knowing Ed wouldn't return as long as he was there. We kids knew where Ed was but didn't say anything. Dad and Ed came back together the next morning and I was surprised to see that dad wasn't angry; in fact, he seemed to be proud of the spunk Ed had shown in running away.

Our family was very poor at this time. Dad built boats and was apprenticing for carpenter papers. But when I was five, he just upped and left us, going north to fish. After that, he rarely came home and never sent mom any money. So things got even worse than before. With their marriage practically broken off, mom had to earn a living for all of us. Granddad helped mom with the crab shack business she ran with my dad. Ed and granddad caught the crabs at night and watched us kids while mom pounded them during the day. She would then go around selling them, and that's how we managed to get a little money.

It wasn't long, however, before my younger brother Gordon was born. Mom couldn't work for a time after that, and by the time she could, granddad was too old to trap. So mom did both jobs, working night and day, trapping and pounding. But after a while this got to be too much for her and she had to stop. We kids were getting older and started helping out. Ed got a paper route and made about eight dollars a month when he was only eight. When Roger reached that age they started caddying at Capilano Golf

Course. Both boys went caddying on Saturdays and Sundays and usually brought in ten or twelve dollars a week. When I turned seven I started taking in washing and ironing for Whites in the neighbourhood. Sometimes we went to the nearby Indian Reserve and played with the kids there ... but not often because we usually had so much work to do at home. Every summer mom planted a garden. We all worked in it and some of the vegetables lasted us into the fall.

There was always a lot of talk in the neighbourhood about my mom — how she used to run around and all that. Only Ed and my youngest brother are dad's kids. When dad was gone, people were always trying to break into the house. I remember one night when a guy broke in; mom had a wood chopping axe and was standing by the window telling him to get out or she would chop his head off. He finally left, but I dreamed that night that mom had killed him. I woke up in a sweat.

The community we lived in was really very strange ... weird things were always happening. An uncle of ours lived about a mile away. Time and again he came over and stole our skiff and sold it to a man named Sebastian. Whenever it happened, mom walked over to Sebastian's place about two miles away and got it back. But they always argued fiercely. Once mom went over with an axe: she was bent on really fixing him for buying the skiff again, which he knew was ours. Actually, the skiff was over at his place a lot.

When Sebastian saw her steaming down the trail with an axe he panicked and called the police. When mom got there he backed off yellin' that the police were coming. She just took the skiff and went home. She locked up the house and we all hid in closets. Sure enough, the police came and banged loudly on the door. We didn't answer. They then

25

broke into the house and looked around, but didn't find us. I remember being really scared that mom would be taken away to jail.

Most of the people we knew lived on the Indian Reserve. The people outside the Reserve in our neighbourhood were mainly squatters, living on houseboats or shacks on the mud flats. There were a few large families like ours, but most were smaller. Some of the men worked as longshoremen and others collected welfare — about half and half. Then there was one man who worked as an electrician and another who repaired radios. Both families had two kids, but for a very long time they didn't let them play with us. I guess it was because of mom's reputation.

Six families, most on welfare, lived in boathouses built up on stilts. The dredger's house was on stilts too, but it was really nice. He was from South Africa and his wife was mulatto. She talked a lot about the racism back home — about how they'd had to leave because her husband, a white, had married a coloured woman. They moved into the neighbourhood when I was four and I played a lot with their son, Brian. I didn't know what Blacks were then; I just knew they were different, much friendlier to us.

Another family lived between our house and the Reserve. The father worked until they discovered he had a tumour in his head. Once it was removed he couldn't balance himself well, so the family was forced to go on welfare.

Then there were the Reids, who owned the local store. They were really mean to all the neighbourhood kids. Sometimes when we walked into the store Mrs Reid would throw us into a big barrel filled with lizards. Her life was miserable — always mean and fighting with her husband. They were always drinking and getting into car accidents. Once they even drove through our woodpile and smashed into the house.

There was also a Canadian Indian-Mexican family nearby. Gracie Flores, the daughter, spent some time looking after us kids when mom went away for a few days. Then there was Jimmy Waddel. His family lived above the store and his father worked at McKenzie Barge and Derrick, a boat-building outfit. Jimmy and the older Korris boy down the street always picked on my brother and the younger kids from the Reserve. Whenever we played they tried to bully us around. So one day we decided we'd had enough. It was quite funny. Ten of us little kids were making faces at Jimmy from around the corner of a house, calling him "dirty old man," "whitey," "white boy," and things like that. We had this huge chain from a logging boom with us and when he chased after us we all hid behind a tree. He could see us, of course, but when he ran up we wrestled him to the ground. Then we took a big padlock from dad's boatshed and chained and locked him to the tree. The chain was real heavy, so he couldn't get away. We just left him there crying.

That night Mrs Waddel came over to tell my mother that Jimmy was lost. She was weeping. Jimmy was only eleven. I didn't think much more about it until the police came. Suddenly I wondered if anyone had unlocked him. I was only five and didn't have the key. All of us kids kept quiet. Ed didn't know. He was older and we knew he would tell on us. Next morning they finally found Jimmy. He was still crying and told them the whole story — except who had done it. After that he never bothered us little kids again.

When I turned seven I had my first birthday party. I got a skipping rope and remember really enjoying it. We didn't skip with it much, though. We would have fun tying it around Roger, me and my little sister, Joan, who was very small for her age, five, about the size of a three-year old. Bound together, we would run down the hill as fast as we could. Joan couldn't keep up and usually ended up being dragged along. Once she got caught in the bushes and got scratched. She was usually screaming about something, so we didn't pay any attention; just kept yelling back, "Come on Joan! Keep running!" Finally we realized how hard it was becoming to pull. Looking back we saw we'd been pulling little Joan through the thick brambles. She was covered with cuts and bruises and crying loudly. We promised her all sorts of favours and she promised not to tell mom. At home she said she'd fallen into the bushes, but mom didn't believe her. It was the first time I got a spanking from my mom.

The next came when I lost a new pair of shoes that the Campbell family had given me. We were playing in the old sawdust pits, jumping into them from a high crumbling wall. Joan put my shoes down and they disappeared into this little hole. We dug for them, but the walls of the hole kept caving in. Then we got a shovel and held Joan upside down by the feet while she dug deeper and deeper. But we couldn't find them and almost dropped Joan on her head. Finally we gave in and told mom. She spanked us good, mainly because she didn't want us down at the sawdust mill. She got so angry, she sprained a finger. It swelled up so bad she couldn't spank Joan, but Roger and I spanked her good because we figured she was the cause of our problem and deserved a good one.

Soon after this incident, mom became very ill — or at least it seemed so to me. I was very worried. I thought it was my dad's fault that she was dying because he wouldn't take her to the hospital. I decided I would shoot him ... he was just no good, I thought. All he could say was that he didn't have enough money to take mom in, but we knew it wasn't true because he was a pretty good fisherman. I knew about death because we had done a lot of duck hunting and fishing. I thought it wouldn't be difficult to shoot dad. I told Roger my plan — he was eight then — and he talked me out of it, saying "If mom dies, shoot him. But let's wait and see — otherwise it's just stupid." Well, I agreed — somewhat afraid to go ahead with my plan anyway — and mom got better in a couple of weeks. You have to understand that I really loved mom, and I hated my dad — especially when I was a young kid.

For a long time, dad had only been coming home occasionally, then one day he moved back in and said to us kids that he was going to stay around awhile. Actually, he started being quite nice to us. My earlier hatred melted and I even began to like him a little. He got a job with Sterling Shipyards and continued to fish, taking Ed along with him. He wanted to take Roger too, but he was only eight and couldn't pass for twelve, which was the minimum legal age for fishing.

One day when Roger and I were down at the waterfront, he said: "Babe let's take the skiff and go see dad; he's fishing down at Rivers Inlet." I said "Okay," and he ran to the crab shack to get the oars. It was locked, but we were determined to go by now and "borrowed" a pike pole and paddle from Allen George's canoe on the beach. We knew what we were doing was wrong. Mom and dad had both told us not to play around the water. We'd taken the boat out without asking several times — sometimes for hours — and mom and dad would worry, telling us how dangerous it was when we finally returned. Nevertheless, we pushed the heavy skiff over some barnacles down to the shore. We didn't know it, but we'd scraped up a few small holes in the bottom. Paddling and poling, we headed up the coast and out toward the ocean, bailing water all the time. After travelling about five miles, we found ourselves at the mouth of the inlet near Lion's Gate Bridge. We couldn't paddle beyond the point no matter how hard we tried. Finally, the ocean current settled us onto the shore. Long hours of paddling and poling had convinced us it was time to go home. But how were we going to get the skiff back? We sat there a long time trying to figure it out: "Should we leave the skiff and walk back? Or try to make it back against the current, tired as we were?" As we talked it over, an RCMP patrol boat pulled up. The police asked us a few questions, then towed us home. Mom was worried finding us missing and the boat gone and had phoned the RCMP after a few hours. At home Roger just kept crying, saying he'd really wanted to visit dad up at Rivers Inlet. Mom told him we'd only gone five miles and it was another 300 to Rivers Inlet. But Roger was still too young to understand much about miles, so the tears kept falling. I was tired and didn't care anymore about Rivers Inlet, just wanting to lie down and rest.

In 1959, when mom became pregnant again with my younger brother, dad left home for good. He yelled at mom, saying she was whoring around with other men, havin' kids that weren't his, and so on. Maybe he was right, but he fooled around plenty too. Since 1947 he would be leaving her for six months to a year at a time. Sometimes she talked to us about how bad it was being without a man in the house, and what it was like when they had no kids. She said Nelson died because dad refused to take him to the hospital — and she would never forgive him for that. Then when he was home they argued and fought a lot about Nelson, Ed and me. Dad just didn't like Ed and kept complaining that I wasn't even his kid. He accused mom of telling us stories when he was gone, trying to make us hate him. But in fact, mom remained loyal to him until long after he'd left her, always telling us he was a good man who just had too many troubles.

Around this time a girl named Karen Thomas — we called her "Toni" — came to live with us. She'd been working in the canneries but was continually being laid off because of strikes or shortages of fish. So she decided to look after us kids while mom worked. She became like an older sister. We would often sit around in the evening and have long discussions — mainly mom and Toni. Sometimes they'd talk about politics. You see, when I was seven mom joined the Communist Party. Two years later there were lots of conflicts and she dropped out. I never found out why, except her saying the communists were real creepy, but since then she's been anti-communist.

With dad gone, we began working after school and didn't have much chance to play. When I was nine I started taking care of my baby brother in the summer while mom worked at the Army & Navy Department Store. She'd always been at home before and now we felt lost without her. We just couldn't understand why she had to go off to work every day and I remember our telling her in childish anguish that we would all work harder if she stayed at home. I was taking in ironing and doing a little baby-sitting outside, but we couldn't make enough to live on. She had a deeply held ethic, handed down from both her family and dad's father, that people ought to work. Government was always trying to put Indians on welfare, but they didn't want it. Government said they were going to take away Indian trapping and fishing rights and put them on welfare — the Indians resisted. Our grandparents had been involved in many anti-welfare struggles.

With mom, it was partly a matter of pride; she didn't

want her folks to come out and see her living like that ... on government handouts. She would sometimes cry and talk to me, saying she couldn't understand how it was we could work so hard and yet be so poor ... and grumbling under her breath that she would never accept their dirty welfare money. So we all worked very hard at the crab shack and various other jobs. Mom was nearly forty and was having a very difficult time carrying George. Once she had been crying and sick for about two days. I cried too. We were very close then. She asked over and over, "Why are we so poor when we work so hard?" She was just talking out loud, but I felt she was asking me and I didn't have an answer. I just wondered alone with her how it was that no matter how hard we worked — my brothers caddying or doing other odd jobs, me ironing, etc. — we never seemed to have anything to eat but the fruit and vegetables we canned. We almost never bought anything. I never wore a regular pair of shoes till I was ten — only runners — and we never had any heat in the house. I also began wondering why most people — white people — didn't like Indians and treated us badly, like we weren't as good as they were. And soon I began to wonder if, or how, we could change the situation we found ourselves in. We seemed to be caught in the same rut all the time ... always runnin' around in the same miserable rut. But I was still far too young and inexperienced to understand the social and class nature of our oppression.

A couple of years later, when I was eleven, mom bought another house. She was one of the few people in the neighbourhood who owned their own place. We got $15,000 for the old house and lot — and I was really happy to leave the mud flats. I always seemed to be sick in that house, with no protection against the cold, wet winters and the wind which constantly whipped in off the ocean. Things got a lot better when we moved into the new place. It had a furnace and central heating. Some of our friends from the Reserve helped us move, but we girls did most of the work as the boys were out fishing.

Then my mother began to change ... for the worse, I thought. She quit drinking, stopped running around with men and became very moralistic. But what was bad was that she stopped being the easy-going person we all loved and enjoyed being around. Actually, we thought she was going a bit crazy. She sat and stared a lot, talking to herself and acting in other strange ways. A certain tension filled the house and it scared all of us.

Because mom wanted me to, I started studying the Bible ... but I didn't like it. It was full of unbelievable fantasies. As a kid, I thought a lot, but never daydreamed or fantasized. My dreams were mostly of conversations I'd had; I'd remember things that happened and try to figure them out. I was always trying to understand things — why there was air, how we breathed, and so forth. There was something in me that made me conscious of all the little things that happened.

Three months after I entered school I became aware that I was an Indian and that white people didn't like me because of the colour of my skin. I talked about it with kids on the Reserve but they would just say "We don't like whites either." Even the older people didn't like whites. Many worked in the white communities, around white people, but they had no white friends. Like most of the kids, when some white called me a name or abused me, I fought back. But otherwise I just ignored them like everyone else, fighting their contempt with silence. Of course, my situation wasn't simple because my old man was white. But when he got drunk and angry with mom he called her a "dirty old squaw."

By the time I was nine I didn't want anything to do with whites. There were many in my school, but I had no friends and asked no questions in class. When a teacher called on me I just refused to answer. As time went on I became very nervous and uncomfortable at school; I just wanted to be completely away from white people in my daily life. A talent I had in art added to my misfortune. I once made a clay bear and glazed it black, but it came out gray. I tried again, but still it came out gray. My teacher was nice to me and sympathetic. He took my bear around to the other classes and talked about how well it was done. The kids took notice and some told me they really liked it. Of course, I remained passive. I didn't want their compliments, or even to be noticed. I wanted only to be left alone, ignored. Their attention just embarrassed me, and my hatred of that bear grew monstrous in comparison to its size. Because of it I was drawn into the Whiteman's spotlight — a place I wanted to avoid. But I silently accepted the situation — their tolerance, their racism.

After we moved, I went to a new school in Lynn Valley. I remembered that standing up and being introduced to my new class was — after the bear incident — the second most humiliating incident in my life to that point. The teacher then appointed a girl to show me around the school. I really needed it too; I'd become completely introverted, keeping all to myself and rarely talking. My problem was complicated because it was around this time that mom started talking to herself, flying off the handle at nothing, and forgetting things all the time. I thought a lot about it and decided that I didn't ever want to become like her. In fact, I'd reached a point of not wanting anything more to do with either mom or dad. We'd been very close before, mom and me, but now we seemed very far apart.

There was another new girl in my school, named Gertrude. I'd known her in grade two. When I was little I always wanted hair like hers, long and very blonde. Sometimes she teased me saying, "Don't you wish you had long pretty hair like mine?" It made me very sad and angry. Then one day I was playing with her hair; she'd let me do it because it flattered her. We were in school. Then, as I braided the long blonde strands, I added some of dad's boat glue, which I kept in my desk. I worked it carefully into the braids and by recess they had become hard as a rock. When Gertrude jumped up to flaunt her pony-tail, it swung around and hit her like a stick right in the face. She screamed, then started crying. I was taken to the principal, who gave me a hard strapping. They told mom, but she didn't get angry; in fact she thought it was funny and laughed. "Maybe that'll teach her not to bug you anymore," she said. By grade six, Gertrude had become a really vain and mean person, but she never bothered me again.

After a time in the new school I started to change a bit. I became a little more relaxed around white people. One of my teachers was a pretty nice guy. I remember reading about various religions and talking to him about why people believed in these strange ideas. He had been to the Soviet Union in 1956 and was a liberal — not at all anti-Russian. I decided that I would like to go visit Russia too. When mom was in the Communist Party she'd subscribed to a magazine called "Soviet Union," published in Moscow. Sometimes all of us kids would sit around and talk about what we saw and thought. I remember liking the photographs very much — especially the ones of Eskimo dwellings. The idea that they were all alike fascinated me.

This Mr. Cleamens was also my music teacher. He asked why I never sang with the rest of the kids in the chorus. When I didn't reply, he said that if I didn't start singing he would have me stand up in front of the entire class and practice so I would overcome my shyness. But I remained silent in the chorus. Finally, he told me to stand and sing before the class. I don't remember if I uttered a few notes or not; just that I started crying and didn't go to school for the next three weeks. I've never been able to sing ... can't even carry a tune. After I returned he allowed me to remain silent. Strangely enough, our choir won several prizes that year.

In grade six my marks improved for the first time. I was a straight "A" student that year and the next. I also became good friends with a Jewish classmate named Maria von Strassen. Once I even went to synagogue with her. But I decided I didn't want to become Jewish — or any other religion for that matter.

Maria, however, was a very nice girl, and very quiet. Everyone used to pick on her because of her being Jewish, quiet and a good student ... I guess. Anyway, I often walked to school with her even though the other girls didn't want anyone to play with or talk to her. Once a gang of them came down on me as I walked to school. They started calling me names and beating up on me. I became furious and ferocious, screaming that if they didn't stop I'd kill them all, one by one. "I'll get every last one of you!" No matter how long it takes me! I'll kill you all!" I yelled. But that just made them madder. They sat on me and punched my arm and stomach very hard. I was sick for a couple of days after and wore sweaters so mom and the others wouldn't find out what happened.

A few days later we were playing softball at school. The biggest girl, the one who started the fight with me, was pitching. When I came to bat I really whacked the ball and it hit her right smack in the stomach. She fell down, unconscious, while all her friends came rushing in to beat me up again, yelling that I'd done it on purpose. "You're bloody right," I yelled back, "and if you come closer I'll smash you with this bat!" As they moved in, I swung the bat around and nearly hit one of the girls in the head. Someone ran in to get the principal while one of the girls who hadn't been involved in the matter said, "No one is going to hurt you Bobbi. Why don't you give me the bat and let's forget it?" "Get away," I said, "or I'll knock your head off too!"

The tension was building, but nothing else happened. The girls just drifted away, knowing I was very serious. Then the principal came out and talked to us. From then on, whenever there were parties, the girls made sure to tell me I wasn't invited ... and when our class went on biology field trips, or to the zoo and so on, nobody would walk with me. The other girls started easing off her and she even made some new friends. This really made me cynical. It was the first time in my life I'd been open to friendship with white girls, and now their contempt and ostracism forced me to conclude that all whites were the same: creepy, cruel racists that I wanted nothing more to do with.

As far as school was concerned, I didn't even want to go anymore. I would often drink mustard with water, getting a bit sick in order to stay home. Mostly, I just left the house and, instead of going to school, took long walks down the canyon or out in Stanley Park. Even in winter I went up to the swamp and hiked — sometimes with my brother, sometimes alone. At times we hiked into the water shed and guards would come and chase us off. Then we sometimes saw bears and ran away. Around our new house the bears were really strange; sometimes they came right into the yards looking for food. Once there was a knock on our door and mom hollered, "Come in! Come in!" but no one entered. Then more knocks and more "Come in's." Finally though we rarely ever opened our door personally for visitors, mom went and pulled it open with a swish of frustration. Standing there on his hind legs was a huge bear. I wanted to laugh and scream at the same time. Mom was so frightened she just stood there for an instant, her mouth open; then she slammed the door and ran around locking all the doors and windows ... as if the bear was bound and determined to come in. Instead, he just ran away ... probably as scared as we were.

Later, we had other troubles with bears. My younger brother, George, was three and often went to play in a nearby fruit orchard. One day I walked down through the trees looking for him. Suddenly, I found him playing peacefully with two small bear cubs. I'd heard how fierce mother bears became in defense of their cubs and ran home as fast as I could to tell mom. She told me to get him immediately. Luckily, there was no sign of the mother bear yet and I grabbed George and pulled him all the way back to the house. When more people moved in, the bears slowly left the area. But that was much later.

Squirrels were more fun. We kept them around the house by feeding them ... almost like pets. We also had a racoon, but he was pretty wild.

Sometimes dad came to visit us and often paid the house bills. There'd be a lot of tension in the atmosphere, but no serious trouble that I can remember. My negative feelings toward him eased off, but there was still little emotion in our relationship. In the wintertime he stayed at the house and slept downstairs. Mom slept upstairs with us kids. They didn't live together; just shared the same house. We would put up with him, more or less, till he left again for who knew how long.

Early Rebellion

I barely managed to pass grade eight — more by chance than merit or hard work. Then in the summer our old man got a Veteran's Land Act loan (or mortgage) and we built a brand new house. We cultivated a half-acre of land nearby and planted a garden in the small orchard that was there. We girls helped dig and transfer soil, but after that all we did was tend the orchard and harvest the cherries and other fruit. It was nice then, especially during the summer.

After the house was built, dad started working for a fishing company. I got a job as a live in baby-sitter for a family in South Vancouver and mom had just finished a year at nurses' training school and was saving for the next. We were counting on help from the old man, but he didn't contribute much. Can't blame him a lot, though. The company he worked for never paid their workers till the end of the fishing season.

About three weeks before school was about to begin again, mom phoned and asked if I could loan them five dollars; they'd been living on potatoes and spinach from the garden for over a week. I went home on Sunday and gave them forty dollars — most of my savings. When school started I didn't have enough money to pay for book rentals. I had registered at the Argyle Secondary School, but now was too poor to go. I wasn't really upset; school hadn't left me with many fond memories, so it was fine to think of never going back.

Eventually, however, Welfare stepped in and paid the school fees for all of us. Mom felt ashamed to accept their money, and was very angry with dad because of it. They had a big fight and she yelled at him, "If you're workin' why is it you can't feed the kids and pay their school fees?" After the fight, dad left us and lived most of the time on his boat — just coming back to visit us at Christmas time. He was much different than mom; taking welfare didn't bother him a bit anymore. He was a quiet man ... never talked very much. The only time I really enjoyed him was when he got a little drunk and would sing and play his guitar. Then he was full of jokes and laughs. After the fishing season was over, in 1963, dad started working for MacMillan-Bloedel up at Powell River. He would come home every couple of weeks or so, give mom some money, and head back to work.

In the beginning I was one of the top students at Argyle Secondary, getting all A's and B's during the first semester. I did it more or less to prove something to myself. Kids used to say I was dumb, but I knew that I wasn't. Not caring isn't being dumb — I knew I was intelligent and could get the grades if I tried. After about half a year, however, I soured on school again. I had few friends and found the work boring. So I just about stopped going, missing 72 days of classes during the school year.

Earlier someone told me that if I joined the track team I could get out of some classes and detentions — which was the way they punished us when we played hooky. So I decided to run track and won my first race against the Kensington team. Then I went on to compete in the Vancouver Area School District Games, which involved 52 schools. I entered the 440, 880 and mile senior women's races. When I won all three I was really surprised; I hadn't competed much before then and had no idea how I'd do against good competition. It was a great feeling to win, and it qualified me for the B.C. Championships, which were held at Brockton Oval in Stanley Park. I entered four races, coming in third in the 220 and first in the quarter, 880 and mile. At 14 I'd become the B.C. champion in women's distance races.

Soon, however, I started having real trouble with my back; it was from a roller skating accident I'd had a year earlier. I saw a doctor and he put me on heat treatments and other kinds of physiotherapy. But it didn't work; I still had backaches all the time and was forced to give up track. I was really getting sick of school at the time, anyway.

Sometimes I played hooky for one or two weeks at a time. Mom didn't find out about it until later. She was back at nurses' training school and all I had to do was keep the house clean. So one day I put a baby-sitting ad in the newspaper and soon, instead of going to school some days, I began baby-sitting for various people. Then in January, I got a job in the evening at a restaurant where my brother was working. This only lasted a month or so, however, as the Labour Relations Board found out that I wasn't sixteen yet and told the manager he couldn't employ me in any capacity.

When summer came I turned fifteen and started baby-sitting for the Martin family. They didn't live far from us, so I stayed at home nights and took the bus back and forth to their house. Mrs Martin paid my bus fare plus five dollars a day. She had two kids — a boy about three and a girl, Elissa, who was eighteen months old and had epilepsy. She would be okay, then suddenly become paralysed. They took her to all sorts of doctors even the Mayo Clinic in New York, but no one could figure her out or help. I had to walk around with her because sometimes she would become paralysed and fall on her face. It was a hard job and I really felt sorry for the kid and her mother.

43

During this time, some guy kept coming to the Martin's apartment and knocking at the door. I never answered or opened the door. Then one day I saw him molesting the little girl down the street. I called the police and they caught him. Turned out he had already raped and murdered two young girls twelve and thirteen, the Rainee sisters. It used to scare me to think about it — and about how close I came several times to opening the Martin's door.

Not long after this, my brother and I started to steal things, small things, but we kept at it. We'd take cartons and boxes of cigarettes from big stores and sell them for two-bits a pack. Soon we'd become typical delinquents. I wasn't giving money to my mom anymore, just using it for my own pleasures. I didn't care about the others; I was just for myself, nothing else mattered. I also started smoking, but not around mom — who didn't know. I began with just a couple of cigarettes a day, but quickly went up to around a pack as my stealing increased. I often baby-sat at night, or would go downtown to the nightclubs. I was still only fifteen, but looked much older than my age.

I remember the first time I got drunk. It was down at the Pacific National Exhibition (PNE) Playland with my sister, Toni. She was twenty-one and bought a "mickey" of whiskey for me ... it didn't bother her that I was only fifteen. In fact, she didn't have moral qualms about anything. I went into one of the bathrooms and drank it all down. Next thing I remember I was out of the PNE down near some sawmill. I was running along, holding a big bottle of beer, and some guys were chasing after me. I guess I'd stolen it from them and was pouring it out as I ran, laughing as they yelled. I somehow lost them — or they just stopped coming, seeing the beer spilling over the ground — and went into a store and bought a coke. I didn't drink it, just spilled it on the counter. Then I went out and was really feeling good. There was still some beer left in the bottle I was carrying and I drank it down.

The guys who'd been chasing me spotted me again, but I lost them and finally wound up back at the PNE. I decided not to pay my way in twice and climbed up and over the fence. A watchman saw me. He caught up with me and took me into a little house. I was really mad. A couple of watchmen had arrived and they were sticking my head under the watertap, putting their fingers down my throat and making me walk around. I kept shouting abuses and swearing, calling them assholes, sons-of-bitches, and so forth. The watchman was about forty and really seemed to be concerned about me. I hadn't realized how late it was when I climbed the fence — it was about 4 a.m. — and had no idea the PNE was closed. When he took me outside for air and a walk about, I somehow got away from him, climbed back over the fence and ran away. The policemen had been sitting in their patrol car.

Finally, as I was walking across the bridge, some neighbours picked me up. I didn't say anything, but they could see I'd been drinking and was in trouble. I was soaking wet, though it hadn't been raining. To make sure, they asked if I was the Lee girl. (I must have really looked something else.) I said "Yes," and they drove me home. It was five in the morning when I climbed into bed. Mom didn't say anything, though I knew she heard me coming in.

It was about four months later when I told mom I wanted to go to a dance in town. She got angry and told me not to go ... it wasn't a place for young girls. I was set on going anyway and while she was in the kitchen, I snuck out the window and went into town. When I came home it was late and I crawled right into bed. Mom wasn't sleeping, however. She came into my room, dragged me out of bed by the hair and gave me a good beating. My sister Joyce was crying and Joan kept asking mom to stop. But she was furious: just kept pulling me around the room by my hair and screaming at me. I thought she was going crazy. She kept yellin' "Cut it out! Smarten up!"

I didn't get along with my mother after that incident ... practically broke off relations with her altogether. And I kept going out whenever I wanted, not even telling her I was leaving, or where I was going. Sometimes I'd stay away for a couple of days and not even call. I hung around mostly with Toni, then later with a cousin from Deep Cove who was sixteen. We met a group of guys and I started going around with one of them; a great big guy named Rich. Then I went around with Nigel for a while. I was like that: fickle, intense, always on the move.

School had practically dropped out of sight: I rarely went and when I did was always getting into trouble. Several times they threatened to expel me, but mom kept calling up and talking them out it, saying I had problems but would settle down soon ... things like that. By this time, mom was a practical nurse; she'd worked hard and completed her schooling. I kept telling her I'd be good, promising to go to school regularly and so forth. But then I'd fall back into my old habits. My brother Roger was doing the same thing — in fact, he was worse that I was, attending only about half his classes. Somehow, I barely managed to pass Grade Ten.

It was a really bad time for me. There was this one teacher who was always getting on me about my playing hooky and just being a "visitor" to his classes. Then one morning I was late, my back was aching, and he came on with the same stuff, saying, "Ah, here's Bobbi, our visitor" ... Well, for some reason, I just flipped out; something snapped in my head and I started crying and throwing desks around. I even threw one at the teacher and turned over his table. In a few minutes some teachers came in and grabbed hold of me, dragging me down to the nurses' station where I was given a bunch of tranquilizers. They sent me home after I'd calmed down.

For the next week or so I just stayed home, crying all the time and not wanting to do anything. Finally, my mom decided to take me into the hospital for a check-up. They put me in a psychiatric wing of Lion's Gate Hospital in North Van for three weeks of forced rest. The doctors told me I'd had a nervous breakdown and, with a little rest, would soon be all right. I was pretty upset about being put in a psychiatric ward and was very uncooperative at first. They had all these little programs for the patients and I refused to participate in any of them. A girl down the hall was also uncooperative and my first afternoon in the hospital she tried to escape. They caught her sneaking down the stairs and she fought like a wild cat with the nurses. They finally calmed her down with some injections and the next morning she went sent off to Riverview Mental Hospital.

One of the first year nurses, who'd known my brother in school, said they'd send me off to Riverview too if I didn't start cooperating. This scared me a bit so I decided to start playing their stupid games. On the third morning I went to what they called occupational classes. They had us crushing egg shells and I started complaining, saying, "What good is crushing these egg shells? That won't get us jobs anywhere!" I was warned again by the young nurse: "If you keep complaining like that," she said, "they'll probably send you to Riverview for three months. You'd better play it cool so you can get out of here and go home soon." It took me almost a week, but finally I decided to do everything they asked or wanted without question or complaint. The tranquilizers they gave me four times a day helped; I was dozing or spaced out most of the time and was given sleeping pills at night.

I saw a psychiatrist three times while I was at Lion's Gate and, despite the fact that he kept telling me I'd just had a nervous breakdown — which was very common — I was pretty disturbed by the whole experience. I didn't think I was crazy and resented being kept in the psychiatric ward. Anyway, after three weeks they sent me home with a prescription for tranquilizers which I was supposed to take regularly and get renewed every three months. I was also supposed to see this psychiatrist they set up appointments for me with. I rarely took the tranquilizers and never went to see the psychiatrist. At home I just tried to forget the whole thing. I started school again, switching from the Sciences to the Humanities and taking English, French and Drama.

I did pretty good in Drama, because I liked it, but did poorly in everything else. Acting helped me overcome my shyness and get outside myself. It helped me a lot. I started talking to people and making friends. One was Donna Wooten, a girl who was very similar to me. Her father was very mean, always beating up on her. She told me he didn't like Indians, and neither did the rest of her family. Her brother would sometimes come up to us and make like he was a TV Indian doin' a little dance and saying "Hoo, hoo, hoo." And that was pretty typical. Sometimes we'd make friends with white kids, then they'd tell us after a while to stop coming over because their parents didn't want Indians around the place. I remember going to this girl's house — she was my first friend at school and very nice — and when her mother saw me she blew her stack. Right in front of me she said: "What do you think you're doing bringing this Indian into the Lynn residence? Don't you know we don't want Indians here!" The poor girl started crying — just didn't know what to do or say. Guess she never knew that her folks were like that. You know, like when you're eleven and watch TV stuff about cowboys and Indians you just don't associate that racist crap with your own existence or with your parents' attitudes; it's just exciting and something to do after dinner. Well, after that experience I thought a lot about just taking that sort of thing — letting it just happen to me without doing anything. I started being a bit arrogant and found that the more cocky I was, the more racism came out ... and I was glad when it did because I didn't like phoniness. I like people to be sincere, not the usual phoney and paternalism. Anyway, Donna Wooten was different from the other whites I knew — except for Glenn Hampton, who was also a friend of mine for a very long time. (I think he's a mechanic now somewhere in Vancouver, though I never see him anymore.) Donna and I were real close. She was raised in Quathiasca Cove right next to the Indian Reserve and, in fact, seemed very much like an Indian herself. We stuck together despite her parents' protest and the trouble it caused with the other white kids at Arglye and in the neighbourhood. She'd say that in Quathiasca all her friends were Indians anyway — so what? But at Quathiasca there were no white kids to be friends with.

I remember noticing around this time, when I was fourteen or fifteen, that my sister Joyce was really different than me. She got along with everybody very well, but I thought she was a "yes girl"; always saying "Oh, yes, you're much smarter than me. Yes, of course. Yes, yes." And always walking like she was ashamed, around white guys. It seemed to me she just accepted being a second-class citizen,

49

With California Farmworkers

In May 1966, just before I turned sixteen, mom kicked me out of the house. I had become just too much for her to handle. I wouldn't help out at home, didn't answer when she spoke to me, played hooky from school a lot and was always running around. It was really getting bad for her, so she kicked me out. I lived with friends in North Van for a few weeks, saw Donna a couple of times, then left for the States to stay with Toni, who'd gotten married and moved to a town in California called Visalia. It was a long, 1,100-mile bus ride which ended about 400 miles south of Fresno.

That first night I met Toni, her husband Arturo Ramirez and her brother-in-law, Lorenzo. Arturo was Mexican, and I had known him since I was a little kid. He lived near us in Vancouver and started going around with Toni when he was eighteen and she was sixteen. Mom liked him. He taught her Spanish and learned some French from her. They both would say it was better knowing two languages than one. Arturo was in the navy for two years, but kept coming back to visit. When he got out, he worked in Seattle and came up every weekend to be with Toni. They got married when she was 21, five years after they'd started going around together.

Lorenzo, Arturo's brother, was nineteen and worked in the grape fields. "Mama" Ramirez owned two acres of an old walnut grove which had been split up and subdivided many times. She had some walnut trees, a garden plot and some of the old workers' cabins that had never been torn down. Lorenzo lived in one of these. It was pretty nice; kind of built up on stilts over a tool shed, but nothing tremendous. We talked a lot that first night and he asked me if I'd stay with him. He seemed like a nice guy — serious, talkative and kind of airy — so I said "Sure ... why not."

Soon Toni and Arturo moved to Porterville, about thirty miles further south. Lorenzo and I stayed in Visalia. There were a few weeks left in the grape season and I started working in the vineyards my second day in town. It was really hard work; you had to pick vines three feet long and heavy with grapes — weighing anywhere from twenty to fifty pounds each — and put them in big crates. So it was really bull work, carrying and loading those heavy vines of grapes into crates all day. We worked from five a.m. till five p.m. with an hour off for lunch — eleven hours — and got paid according to how many crates we loaded. On a mediocre day you could earn maybe five dollars, on a real good day about eight. The temperature in the fields always went up to well over one hundred degrees.

On my first day, at around nine in the morning, I decided to take a break. I crawled under some big vines about four feet tall and before I knew it I was off to sleep. As the sun rose higher my face came under it. I didn't wake up, but boy did I get a bad sunburn on one side of my face. Lorenzo and some others looked for me during lunch, but the vineyard was huge, about a mile wide and at least that deep. They didn't find me till evening, after work. I was a bit dizzy but otherwise I felt okay. At home I went right to bed but later that night I woke up with this horrible headache — felt like I was going to burst right open. All I could do was lie still; when I moved it only got worse. It was like a million dollar hangover, and I thought, "Boy, do I need something!"

This was my first case of sunstroke. I was sick for three

days with this headache but went to work anyway. Everybody laughed at me because one side of my face was burned black as coal. Later, as the summer wore on, I just got darker and darker all over. I always had a craving for water and after work I'd go home and drink till I felt like bursting. We'd usually end up having a water fight. The nearby springs and river were drying up — some were already bone dry by mid-July. There was this one place though that was still hanging in there at the end of July.

When the grape season was over, Lorenzo and I got another job picking. I quit after about three weeks though, as I'd saved up enough to live on and really hated the work. Occasionally we'd pick walnuts for "Mama" Ramirez, and Lorenzo cultivated a small garden near our cabin.

Visalia was really a strange little "Mexican" town. Actually, it was two little towns, with the Mexicans living on one side and the whites on the other. More than half of the population was Mexican, and the rest were white. There were also a few Blacks and some Indians from a nearby Reserve. This was my first experience with really blatant racism. Not that I'd never experienced any racism before — far from it. But here it was so common, so much a part of everyday life, that people never even thought about it. Once, soon after I'd arrived in town, I went into this store and asked a white woman for the time. She just stared right through me; didn't say a word. So I asked some guy and he did the same thing. I began to wonder: "What's going on? Do I have leprosy or something?" Then the owner said, "Get out Mex. No one's got the time for you in here!" It finally dawned on me: "They think I'm Mexican and the racist bastards won't even give me the right time!"

It would have been worse if they'd known I was Indian. The local Indian population lived in really squalid conditions — except for a small elite on the Reserve who lived high on the hog — and were treated worse than Mexicans. In fact, even the Mexicans felt superior to Indians. I thought this was pretty funny, since all the Mexicans were of Indian decent. Of course, they would deny it, saying they were Spanish. It was something they were aware of sometimes — their racism, that is — and would even joke about. But it had become a deeply rooted part of their existence and they just took it for granted. With whites it was the same thing. If a gringo came to the Mexican side of town he would get the same snipe I got: they'd just ignore him; nobody would serve him; he'd be treated like he wasn't there. It was something that would happen to a Mexican on the white side of town. It was just the accepted way of life.

I found this racist scene really strange. Like when I was in the store and a white guy walks in ... probably up from L.A. visiting friends and touring the Mexican part of town. He looked around for a while, then said, "Can anyone help me here?" The Mexican owner just pretended he wasn't there, just went slowly about his business. "Can't I get any service in here?" the white repeated, obviously getting a bit upset. Still no response. The Mexican just slipped further into his stereotyped lethargy; you know, the kind of act we go into when a situation's getting unpleasant. Real slow and nonchalant. I just stood there, confused, until I realised that this was simply a part of everyday life. The Mexicans had gotten so used to racism that it seemed they almost enjoyed it. And it was the same with whites. Every other Saturday night there'd be a dance. Lorenzo's friends would talk him into going — they had a little group that hung around together and they wouldn't go without Lorenzo. I was the first girl that Lorenzo went around with steady, that lived with him, so his buddies would tell him to bring me along. Well, most of the time these dances were just drunken brawls. Some white guys — "okies" and "gringos" they called them — would come over and try to crash the party, take some of the women and beat up a few Mexicans. It was usually a standoff. All the women went home except me; I was always curious and wanted to stay around and see what would happen. It was like a traditional feud, as natural to them as eating or working.

It was different with the small Black population in town. There were just no good "niggers" in Visalia. Whites rarely passed a black man without saying something vulgar to him or his wife. There were always subject to racist attack. Not like the Mexican, who would be passed in the streets as if he wasn't there. I don't know how to say it, but with Mexicans and whites it was more like a reciprocal relationship whereas black people seemed to be subjected to a more one-sided racism. Their reaction to white racism wasn't very strong; they didn't defend themselves and tried not to offend whites. It seemed to me they had kind of a slave mentality, treating whites like they were the bosses. The Mexicans, or most of them at any rate, didn't have that servile mentality. They'd put on their stereotyped slow-motion act, but with them it was a way of fighting back.

With the Indians in town — and elsewhere, for that matter — it wasn't a case of mutual racism. Indians generally think that white people don't like them, so they just don't try to befriend them. They see it as a strange quirk of whites that they don't like Indians — and they accept that as part

55

of their existence. Some, of course, feel a surge of hostility, but it's not a generalized reaction. At least I don't think so.

It's really different with the Mexicans — a different kind of racism. I think it's more insidious, and probably the ugliest, because they're both nonchalant about it. It's not even something that cuts. It goes along low-keyed, then erupts into fights and brawls — like a feud between families in a small town ... Mexicans versus Gringos. You see, Mexicans once owned California as part of Mexico and they feel that even though they were conquered the land really belongs to them. So their feud is like a continuation of the 1848 Mexican War. It's national, cultural and racial all mixed together. Mexicans felt a sense of pride, national pride, fighting the "gringos" for what they thought was rightfully theirs: California. Many of them had originally been brought up to work as "wetbacks" and the fact that they came from Mexico, an independent country, added to their feeling of national pride. In any event, Mexicans reciprocated the racism laid on them by whites.

In Vancouver I'd experienced a similar racial situation, but it wasn't as bad. There, as an Indian, you get those who just ignore you; those who allow you to become only casual acquaintance; and those few whom you can actually become friends with. There are these three types of "other" people, white people, and then there are some who are really vulgar about it, blatant racists. But down in Visalia almost all of them — except for the few who raided parties and started fights — were the type who just ignored you, completely denied your existence.

It took a while for me to get used to life in Visalia. There were a lot of cultural differences. The first two weeks I was there the change in diet gave me constant diarrhoea. I was really miserable, but I didn't tell anyone I couldn't hack the Mexican food — they already hassled me about it. A couple of times I asked for a bite of someone's sandwich expecting it to be peanut butter and jam or something. Then I'd bite into a load of chile pepper relish. I never ate any kind of pepper at home and Christ, I'd be sick for days. I wouldn't say a word, you know, just smiled; but while I was eating the stuff my guts would be on fire. Things like that happened all the time, and when my Mexican friends found out they would joke about it and laugh.

At first I was a bit of a curio to the Mexicans ... a real live Indian from Canada, a place they sort of knew on the map but weren't too sure about. They often gawked at me and said I looked like a Mexican except I was so big. Lorenzo was the same height as me and was tall for the Mexicans down there. They're really pretty short. I was tall and skinny, at least when I arrived. Funny thing is I started putting weight very fast, going from 100 pounds to almost 140 in less than three months. Don't know why. I ate three big meals a day, but did bull work in the vineyards for almost a month. Maybe it was because the work was hot, slow and heavy, where you don't work off any fat, just get tougher and stronger.

When Arturo Ramirez was in the navy and coming up to visit Toni he told us a lot about his home town and what life was like there. But even though I knew a little bit what to expect, I found the change in culture tremendous. Mexicans seemed to me very sociable, yet at times extremely lethargic. They were either really outgoing, light-hearted and fun-loving, or very sombre, dull and bored. At least they had this bored facade they put on for certain occasions. Like in the evenings about five or six o'clock at the house when everyone just sat around bored listening to "Mama" Ramirez talk. She'd just yak away like the older people in other families who didn't work, while the others sat dull and almost asleep. Mexican families seemed to form little cliques; they went around more as family circles than as groups of friends. They were all cousins, aunts and uncles, related in some way or another. This was kind of strange to me because I never hung around with my cousins even though they lived close. In fact, I didn't have much interaction with family and kin at all … not on a social level at least.

Anyway, it seemed weird to me with the kids and everyone listening to "Mama" Ramirez and looking bored stiff. Then there was the language. They'd mostly speak Spanish, which I didn't understand and wasn't interested in learning. Lots of times I felt like a piece of furniture — a table or something — because they'd be speaking Spanish and not caring at all that I didn't know what was going on. I just sat there once in a while someone would say, "Hey, Bobbi, you better learn Spanish." "Oh yeah," I'd reply, "I'll start tomorrow." They really expected me to stay there for the rest of my life, honestly believing that I'd never leave. Because who would ever want to leave Visalia? When I told "Mama" Ramirez that I was leaving all she would say was: "Why you want to leave? Nobody wants to leave here. You're the only one." I'd say, "But I don't come from here; everything's different and I'm getting homesick." "Why?" she'd ask. "You don't like this place? What's wrong with this place?" "Mama" didn't speak much English; she'd never been to school. So I would just say, "Well, it's a fact. I want to go home."

They would often joke and stuff, looking over at me and laughing. I think I was the subject of a lot of their jokes. It didn't really bother me, and there was nothing I could do about it anyway. So I thought, "It must really be funny if they're all laughing so hard," and I'd just laugh with them. Seemed that when they weren't dull and bored listening to "Mama" Ramirez they'd be joking and laughing all the time. I think teasing and ribbing was an important part of their culture.

Sometimes I would joke back at them. In fact, Arturo and I had a joke going for about two weeks. It was really funny. They were curious about life in Canada and we told them we had been living in igloos, describing all the details. Arturo's nineteen-year-old brother was really astounded. "Did you really live in those things?" he'd ask. "Yeah, sure," we'd say. Then Arturo would go on: "I lived in those igloos for a long time when I was in the Navy and working in Seattle." Then we told them that there were no roads, that we travelled by dog team on sleds like you read about in books. "And it's winter up there for ten months a year snowing all the time like crazy."

Finally we told them the truth. Arturo said, "No, don't be stupid. We lived up there just like Americans." "Yeah," I said, "unfortunately. And we don't get much snow; it just rains all the time." Everyone believed us and now they all laughed, especially Arturo and I. So when they laughed at me I didn't mind. Seems that some areas you're naturally sensitive about and others you're not.

Most of the Mexicans in town were farm workers of one kind or another during the summer — mainly in the grape fields. They would get up early, work in the fields until noon, eat, then sleep till three. After their siesta they'd go back to work till five or six. When the season was over they'd get randy or mean when they were drunk. In fact, they didn't fight much among themselves. The men would beat up on their wives pretty bad once in a while, just enough to keep them in their place. They had that old chauvinism about "a woman's place ... " There was also a lot of quarrelling — family spats — and stratification in the family was fairly strong. The man of the family was at the top, then the oldest son, the mother and the younger kids. I didn't like it. Quite often people wouldn't talk to me because I didn't have any status in the family. If a man was talking to his mother you just didn't horn in on their discussion. Sometimes I'd try, when they were speaking in English, but they'd just ignore me or say: "Stay out of this! You're just a little girl."

Another thing that was strange to me was the complaining. They complained all the time; about the ants, the flies, the river, the heat — everything ... except what was really important. They never complained about having to work for five or eight dollars a day or something like that. It was only the trivial things, or something they couldn't do anything about, like the weather. It was always hot in the summer, and always would be. "If you want cooler weather," I would think, "you'll have to move north." But they didn't want to move, just complain. It was the same with things like the meals. They complained about their mother's or wife's cooking. I guess it was just habit, or they enjoyed it. But they'd compliment you on your cooking too, if they liked it, and this seemed a bit strange to me, the complaining on the one hand and the jokes, good humor and compliments on the other.

Mexican kids, like Willy — Lorenzo's cousin — were always spending time in juvenile detention. It seemed to be a big joke to them ... they were almost proud of it. "I went to 'juvie' when I was eight," one kid would say. "Say, that's really great. Keep it up. You know, I've been in four times and I'm only twelve." They usually went in for stealing. They were always stealing ... from each other, from shops,

60

everywhere. It seemed like the normal thing to do. Once I caught a guy who was visiting us walking out with my radio. "Hey," I said, "put the radio back!" He just said, "Okay, you know I was only joking." This is how it was explained. You couldn't get mad because of a thing like that. In fact, if you visited someone else's house you did the same thing. If you managed to get away with it, good. If they came over and saw something you'd stolen from their place they'd just say, "Hey, this is mine. I'm taking it back." The usual reply was, "Sure, that's okay." Then they'd wait for a chance to steal it back.

They also stole a lot from stores — especially the young kids. And they got caught all the time. They weren't slick thieves; they weren't slick about anything. It was just a big joke to them, and an accepted part of life. It was the same with drinking and smoking hash. I did a lot of this myself with Wally, who was only about twelve. We were always smoking or drinking this cheap Tokay wine. Lorenzo used to get real annoyed. He was nineteen but really quite different than the other guys. Even though he was a farm labourer he was sort of an artsy type who never indulged too much in anything. Like he'd drink sometimes, but never get drunk.

Most of the Mexicans kept a few animals — chickens and pigs were really common. "Mama" Ramirez had some fowl and hogs and Wally took a piglet and raised it like a pet. He called it "Arnold" after some television cartoon pig. I don't know how he did it, but he trained this pig to do a lot of things. It was really funny. After a time this Arnold weighed 200 pounds — a bloody big piglet — and would soon grow into a huge hog. Soon it would start breaking the furniture which Wally trained it to sit on. Arnold would sleep on Wally's bed; and Wally used to say, "Okay, Arnold, let's get up!" and the pig would grunt and snort a bit and they'd go watch television. You wouldn't believe it but this Arnold could turn off the television — he'd just whack the knob with his paw. I was always afraid he'd miss and smash the screen, but he never did. Then Wally would say, "Get up on the couch Arnold!" and up he would go. Once the pig ran away or was stolen and I remembered Wally coming in like his world had fallen apart. Arnold was gone for several days, but finally Wally got him back from his Aunt Gracie — "Mama" Ramirez had taken him back thinking he was too pig for a pet.

One time when Wally and I were really drunk on Tokay, this Arnold came in looking for us — or at least it seemed that way. There we were drunk, and still very young, and all of a sudden we're looking at this Arnold who's snorting away like he recognizes us. It was unreal. I was laughing like crazy because the whole situation seemed so unbelievable. The thought kept passing my mind that, "Here I am a thousand miles from home, living with foreigners whom I can barely communicate with, and here's this pig snorting at me like he knows me and I'm drunk as hell." I laughed until Wally stuck my head under the water tap and sobered me up.

When Lorenzo came in he didn't think it was very funny. He had become even more serious than usual, really worried about being drafted. Lorenzo had this whole morality about killing — not only people but even flies and animals. He'd eat pork as long as he didn't have to do the butchering. He'd just received his draft card and would say: "I'm not gonna do any killing for the gringos! And I don't have any illusions about their high soundin' freedom and democracy!"

Once in a while he'd go into the complexities of the war with me, but I wasn't very concerned about it. I just thought, "It's a Vietnamese country, let them haggle over it. If the Chinese want it, let them have it, but the Americans got no right over there." It wasn't a moral question to me — I wasn't anti-communist or pro-communist. It just seemed that they were trying to wipe out the commies and I thought, "Let the Vietnamese do it themselves if they want to. And if they need so much help from America, maybe they should just chuck it." These were my sentiments on the war, but Lorenzo's ideas were much clearer and he knew a great deal more. He said the Americans were just plundering southeast Asia; it was the same as it had been with Mexico, except that Mexico wasn't fighting any more. "The Vietnamese," he would say, "are fighting to keep what's theirs and I don't want to be part of the US machinery to go and kill people and take what's theirs. It'd be like I was a gangster if I went to Vietnam with the US Army — except that I wouldn't even get anything out of it like a regular gangster." Though he stole a lot of stuff around town, he didn't want to be part of the national robbery that was going on in Vietnam.

Lorenzo would tell me all this stuff about the murdering and the napalm, and about racism. He didn't like or accept racism — didn't dislike whites because they were white and thought Mexicans calling white people "gringos" just fed the racism and "wetback" stereotype of the Mexican. But he couldn't see any way out of it. He was quite an unhappy person, I think. Unhappy and discontented. He couldn't understand why racism existed, but he didn't just ignore it or overlook it the way most Mexicans did. They would say, "Sure, we know the gringos are real racists; that's the reason we hate them all." This seemed to be most everyone's attitude, and they really meant it.

But Lorenzo was different, and I guess that's why I liked him. Unlike the other people down there, he didn't have a small town mentality, just thinking about what was happening in Visalia. He thought a lot about what was happening in the world and why. His friends were much different, just like the rest. His relations with them were real superficial, just fooling around a lot, but no really close ties. He mainly tolerated them because they were fun to be with, and I guess they tolerated him because he entertained them. It seemed that most friendships were like that — nothing real serious. You never took your sorrow or discontent outside the family. And any real or deep discontent — not the simple things you complained about — you just kept inside or maybe went to church and confessed about. It was part of their culture.

We talked a bit, but mostly I listened ... not knowing too much about what was going on. Lorenzo was getting into some existentialism, a very individualistic sort of thinking and sometimes we argued about it. But he had read a bit and had the facts while I didn't even read the newspapers at that time. I just wasn't that concerned. And with things like Vietnam, it was always on television and you didn't need much brains to figure out what was going on. Mostly, I just assumed that Lorenzo was tight and accepted his judgement on things. He talked and I listened; not too much dialogue. He talked a lot of philosophy, or at least used the words, and was sort of utopian. He was also an artist and painted a lot ... also thought about a lot of things. He seemed more real to me than other guys I'd known — less superficial. You know, sometimes a person seems more genuine than regular people when they're living in a world of unreality. They're not realistic, but their dreams seem real and sincere.

Anyway, Lorenzo was utopian and I was something of

a cynic. He would talk about the perfect society and place to live and I'd just say: "Look, you know it'll never happen. One thing you have to learn is that you really have to go all out for something you want real bad. You won't make it happen by just sitting and waiting around. What you'll get won't be a dream world. It'll just be a big dream."

But Lorenzo wasn't artificial in the way most of the others were. Most Mexicans there had this stereotyped personality and there were happy with it. They never went beyond their barriers, the social barriers where only the family knew anything about what you were really thinking or feeling inside. I think Lorenzo was more serious about life, thought more about it, and that appealed to me for some reason. People like that had always appealed to me. And it helped me get over some of my cynicism; I didn't want to do anything or take anything serious, but sometimes Lorenzo's utopianism and idealism got to me. He had plans about becoming a mechanic or engineer; he'd change his mind pretty often but he knew he didn't want to be picking grapes all his life or doing nothing and living on welfare. This seemed sort of ridiculous to me, and hard to understand, because I didn't want to work at all and didn't care about getting welfare money.

Well, after a while, Lorenzo started getting real serious about me. He'd talk about us getting married having kids and so on. It kind of scared me. I was too young, I guess; just too unprepared to marry someone like that — or anyone for that matter. It was nice living with him and talking about those things for a while, then I realized I just wasn't really serious about marriage, kids and so on. So I said, "No. I don't want to marry anyone now."

I had been working in the plum fields picking for three weeks when I quit and headed back north. The work wasn't

Problems At Home

When I finally got home after a long and boring bus ride I was really surprised to find that both my brothers had left the house. My sisters had also suffered a terrible experience: one had been raped and the other forced to watch. They were only fourteen when it happened and they still hadn't recovered from the horror of it. So while I was gone it was like my family had been turned upside down or something. They'd even had a bad accident with our car. I was really sad that Roger wasn't there: I was closer to him than anyone else in the family and had missed him a lot when I was down in Visalia. He'd been gone for about two months and no one knew where he was.

I started having a lot of trouble with my back around this time. It was from a roller skating accident I'd had when I was thirteen. Even before going to Visalia I'd had about a year of physiotherapy and all that junk. Now the doctor thought it might be cancer. He sent me to the hospital and they did a bunch of tests — took fluid from my spine and so on. Then they sent me home and I had to wait about two weeks, thinking for sure that's what I had. It was a weird, sort of unbelievable situation. I just couldn't imagine what it would be like to die ... to be dead. I used to think: "Well, it won't be bad. It's just nothing, like sleeping." But I didn't really believe it.

As it turned out, all I had was a minor slipped disk. Still can't figure out why that stupid doctor didn't take an x-ray and find it out earlier. Guess he was morbid about cancer or something. Well, when I was waiting for those test results is when I really missed Roger. I felt I had to find him and see what he was up to. Before I could locate him, however, the police brought him home early one morning. They picked him up in an alley in downtown Vancouver. I guess he'd been living on the skids for a month or so. Anyway, they found him sleeping in this alleyway and thought he was just a young kid. Actually, he was seventeen but was very tiny for his age. He told them his real age but they didn't believe him: thought he was only thirteen or so. They phoned mom and then brought him home. They'd promised Roger they'd tell mom they had found him on the freeway, but when he got home they told her the truth, asking her not to say anything to him about it. It was really a stupid game they were playing — all that lying and deception.

I told Roger about my experiences in the States, especially about how I was struck by the cultural difference. "You don't just integrate into a different culture or atmosphere in three months," I said. "It would take ten years, or even more: you don't realize at first how that difference sets you apart from the rest of the community, makes you a foreigner."

Roger then told me how he'd been trying to get a job, but everybody just laughed at him — all the way from here to Prince Rupert. He applied for over thirty jobs but they just laughed, saying he was too small. They couldn't believe he was more than twelve years old 'cause he was only 4 feet 10 inches tall. This really upset him: I don't think he ever completely got over it. He was in a state of complete depression, knowing he was seventeen but too small to get a job. He said, "What the hell am I gonna do? I'll get older and older but not a hell of a lot bigger. Maybe I'll never be able to get work." I told him not to worry: that his voice was only just changing and he wasn't even shaving yet. But he just looked worried and depressed.

My mom had broken her ankle and when I came back from Visalia she wanted me to get a driver's license so I could drive her around shopping and things like that. Her leg was still in a cast. So I got a learner's permit and then passed my driving test. It wasn't long though before I started being at odds with my family again. I just couldn't take the restrictions imposed by family life — always having to put up with other people and their expectations of me. And there was always this tension; a lot of tension in the household. The atmosphere was so thick with it that I could hardly breath. The old man was back, living downstairs in the basement, and that was a strain too. Mom insisted that I start school again, so I did; but I quit after about three weeks. I began thinking of moving out of the house again, maybe selling a little dope and stuff like that. I was still smoking a bit of grass and hash, nothing fantastic.

I left home after about three months. I didn't want to work but eventually I figured, "There's no way I'm going out of this place if I don't get a job." Mom had really become neurotic. You just couldn't say anything without her yelling, "Why did I ever have you kids anyway?" She was always screaming at one of us, and always complaining about something. It was miserable. So I got a job at an A&W drive-in restaurant and left home. I rented this little room in West Van but moved back home into the house a couple of months later.

The work at A&W was hard; you never had regular shifts. We would work six or eight hours a day — sometimes less, sometimes more, depending on how good we were doing. The boss was an English woman and we didn't get along well. Of all the white people I knew, she was the worst. Most of the other waitresses there didn't like me or the head hostess, who was also an Indian. They'd make nasty remarks about us in the lunch room, usually in whispers or behind our backs. There was one foreign girl there, Lina, from Sweden I think, who always defended us.

This manager was always making me do all the shit work — cleaning up the lot, picking up all the papers and so on. Often she'd have me work up to ten hours a day out in the sun, waiting cars. Sometimes we'd open the joint at 10 a.m. It was never regular. They gave me a little training when I started and a pep talk about the history of A&W. I learned that it was bought from Allan & Wright by the United Fruit Company and that we had to work hard to push the company's food. For about three weeks they taught a bunch of us how to smile and talk to the customers. Then, once we started working, all these inspectors or supervisors would come around to see how we were doing and make reports. Of course, we never knew who they were — just that the reports were coming in about us. There was this feeling of always being harassed by the management to work harder. Once there were only two of us on the lot, me and this Indian hostess. Together we brought in about a thousand dollars for the company, mainly for drinks. It was really a hot day and we worked thirteen hours. Then they expected us to open up the next morning after doing an inventory.

Every day we would have to count up and check our bills, calculating how many regular burgers, cheeseburgers, and so on we'd sold. We'd mark it up and then at the end of the week someone would get a little prize for selling the most cheeseburgers or a compliment for being best hostess. Every Monday we had to do this stupid inventory. It took about an hour and we never got paid for it. They were always shorting us on hours. Sometimes you'd work three hours and get paid for one; if you complained they fired you. A lot of girls got fired for this and other little things, because there were always people around asking for work. At least one girl was fired every month. I worked there six months and the staff had completely changed by the time I left. The Indian head hostess was fired in about my fourth month. After a while I started arguing with the boss because she wouldn't let me take a break after six hours work — which was the law. A few days before I got fired, after she'd refused my break again, I just took it anyway. She ordered me to come see her afterwards and I told her, "Fuck off! Just leave me alone!"

I was getting tired of working there any way. I wanted to become a hippie or something; just do nothing. I wasn't motivated at all; didn't want to work. I figured the world owed me a living: why should I have to work or go to school? Well, me and this Indian cook from Saskatchewan had been working for twelve hours one day and we had to do an inventory that night and open up the next morning. We decided not to, just take off in his car. We drove up to Pemberton, then down to the States and all around. They called from work and asked my mother where I was, but she didn't know. I'd moved down to North Van a few weeks earlier. We went back to work the next day, tired and with bloodshot eyes from not sleeping. Then that weekend we took off again, driving all over the place and talking. He was married and we didn't have any sex. I had been going around with this white guy who was a good friend of his. It was an odd relationship. He was married too and I never liked him to touch me ... maybe because he was white and I just liked him as a friend. Anyway, when this cook and I went back to work they fired us both; just handed us our pay and said, "Get out!"

I stopped going around with this white guy as soon as I left A&W. There was some other guy always hanging around but I never went out with him. Lorenzo kept writing me from Visalia; sometimes I answered but most of the time I didn't. After a while he stopped writing. Not long after losing my job I started going with a guy named Chris; it lasted on and off for about nine months. He was always upset about our relationship. He was divorcing his wife and kept talking about us getting married and stuff like that; but I told him I didn't want to. "You're a nice guy," I said, "and we're having fun, but I just don't want to marry you. And anyway you're drinking too much." He didn't quit drinking, though; in fact it just got worse and eventually I stopped going out with him. I was never very nice to him and maybe that's why he drank so much. I would act mean to him and he'd end up taking me out drinking and to the nicer places I liked. Looking back, I guess I used him to serve my own pleasures.

At this time I wasn't hanging around with Indians — except for Stacy Michaels, an old friend. I was still seeing Donna Wooten, but we weren't as close as before, when we were in school together. Then she started having trouble at home and moved in with me and my sister in North Van. I used to tell her that I hated white people but she'd just say, "I can well understand why." Then she'd go on: "But you're lying, Bobbie. You like me and that doesn't change the colour of my skin." This contradiction bothered me and most of the time I felt I didn't want her living with us anymore. I'd say to myself: "If you don't like white people, how is it that you like Donna?" She really confused me! She was a very open person, letting you know that she wasn't ashamed of being white and didn't think she had any racist sentiments. She could see I didn't hate her and always told me I wasn't being truthful when I said I hated whites.

When we moved into this place it was really filthy ...

with rats and all kinds of junk in it. But we were proud because it was our own "house"— actually it was just a room in a rat-infested old house like the one I was born in. It was small and crowded and the landlady was a real nut. She'd kick us out for having friends over, then forgive us the next morning and ask us to stay. My brother Roger came over a lot and started going around with Donna. That's when I began to feel really close to her again. But liking her a lot made me even more confused about my anti-white sentiments.

Hippie Life-Style 1967

Later, in September 1967, my brother Ed wrote me from Toronto. He'd left Vancouver the year before and now he wrote asking me to go bring him home from Toronto, saying it was urgent: he was hungry and wanted to come home, get a job and so forth. So my mom asked me to go. I said, "Why should I go? Why should I be his keeper?" But she insisted, said she'd pay me back the money if only I'd go get Ed. I had a lot of money at this time, money I'd saved from working and selling dope. Well, finally I agreed. The trouble was that he didn't send us any address, just a postcard from a bookstore on some Yorkville Avenue.

I went to Toronto by bus, I didn't fly. I was afraid to fly. The trip took four days. I took this big suitcase with all my best clothes. I was planning to spend a week or so but ended up staying there almost ten days ... and it seemed like a lifetime. Anyway, I remembered being a little scared: it was a long bus ride and a long way from home. Here I was, sixteen, carrying this big suitcase and walking the streets looking for my brother. At first this guy kept following me, asking if I'd sleep with him. He offered me ten dollars, then twenty. I kept telling him to leave me alone, get lost. Finally I turned on him and yelled, "Just fuck off!" and he did.

I walked around Toronto for two days. I figured that Ed had become a hippie so on the second day I started following this hippie around, walking with my suitcase about ten feet behind her. It was very obvious that I was following her; then she would slow down and so would I. Finally, after I'd followed her around a corner and turned in to York Avenue, she turned and said: "Are you following me?" "Yeah," I said, "I'm looking for my brother and thought you might know where I might find him. His name's Ed Lee." "Ed Lee? He's probably at the Grab-Bag a couple of blocks down the street."

I thanked her. It was two o'clock in the morning and I went into this Grab-Bag. I was really surprised to see Ed sitting there, as if he was just waiting for me to arrive. In fact, he'd been there three days waiting, telling everyone he knew that he'd be there if anyone came looking for him. We talked a while, then I left and started to hitch-hike back to Vancouver. We only got as far as Sudbury, Ontario, when Ed started coming down from drugs, shaking a lot, then getting hot and cold. I think he'd been taking heroin, though he didn't say. He kept getting worse, so finally we headed to Toronto. I thought of going home without him, but he talked me out of it. That night he went out and probably got a fix; anyway, when he came back he seemed fine again.

Next morning he said he wanted to go home. I said "Okay, let's go," and this time we took a bus. He started getting bad again shaking and stuff, but I wouldn't let him get off. He just kept talking crazy and saying he had to go back; just never stopped talking. Ed was real skinny compared to when I'd last seen him. He hadn't been working in Toronto — not a day since he'd arrived. He'd just been pushing drugs and getting hung up on them himself. I'd also been taking grass and hash in Vancouver, and pushing a little, but nothing as bad as Ed. Even before, in Vancouver, I'd become sort of a hippie — with drugs, listening to Bob Dylan music and that stuff. Anyway, I didn't give in to Ed this time and we stayed on the bus straight through to Vancouver. The ten days I'd spent in Toronto seemed a lot longer than that.

After I had turned seventeen, in late September 1967, I got a job at the Inglewood Private Hospital. I just bull-shitted my way into it, saying I was an assistant dietitian. I saw the job listed in the want-ads. Anyway, it was a pretty good job and I learned a lot about diabetic and other kinds of special diets. I picked it up pretty quick. It was connected to this old folks' home and sometimes they'd be short of staff and call me out on the floor ... usually to carry some old man to his bed or something. It was really pathetic; all these little old ladies coming into the kitchen and wanting to help with the dishes, like they were guests or something. They just couldn't get it into their heads that it was a hospital. "You're not visiting your Aunt Lillian," I'd tell them. "You're in a hospital." But they'd still get all balled up in their heads and want to do the dishes, dust or sweep the floor. Sometimes they'd do it and in most cases it was bad for them. They were too sick or old ... that's why they weren't living at home. So I usually put them back in bed, saying things like, "Thanks, but the dishes don't need drying. Anyway, I'm tired, so why don't we go back upstairs and go to bed?" Most of the time they'd say "Okay" and up we'd go.

The main problem was that most of these old folks drank a lot. They came from ordinary working class families and they'd always be sneaking a mick. Sometimes you'd turn around and there'd be this old lady stoned out of her mind. She'd be creating a ruckus or dancing and usually end up falling down and have to be carried back to bed. Sometimes they'd break a leg or get hurt in other ways. It was really dangerous for them to have too much liquor; they just lost all track of how much they could drink. They were so unconscious of reality they'd just keep drinking until it was all gone. I always had to keep an eye out to see that some old gal didn't fall out of bed and crack her skull or something.

I had stopped drinking even before I started work in the hospital, but I was still smoking a little pot and hash. Once a couple of girls asked if I could get them some grass; I did and after that I started pushing a little dope on the side and making some extra money. It got to where I didn't like working in the hospital anymore, but I tried to make the best of it. I didn't want to work at all, but I had to.

Roger started changing a bit after he and Donna got together. He started being a little easier on himself. He'd never been cynical; he was usually optimistic about life and happy-go-lucky, a real nice guy to know and be with. But he was small and got all these knocks looking for a job. Seems he got shit on every time he turned around, he'd be looking for roses and come up with weeds. He was better for a while around Donna, but then he and my old man had a bad scene. He had always been the old man's favourite; he had gotten along with him even though he could see the old man wasn't a good person, would play up to one person at a time and hate all the rest. Roger was usually the favoured one but when he couldn't get a job and started drinking, dad just turned on him with hatred. Roger drank a bit when he was younger but now he really started going heavy, getting drunk all the time and becoming real hostile and punchy. There wasn't much Donna or I could do.

After working at the hospital for about three months, from late September through December, I got bored with my job — and with life in general in Vancouver — and decided to take off with Stacy and go to Edmonton. We took a bus and stayed with Stacy's brother-in-law, a guy named Norman, who was then separated from Stacy's sister. He was really drinking a lot and we started doing the same. Seemed that all we did for about two weeks was drink. Soon after we got there the Children's Aid Society came and took away

78

the kids Norman was supposed to be looking after. I remember the kind of blank look in his face as he was signing them over.

Once we went to this bar and were drinking when Stacy's sister walked in. She really started giving me hell, yelling that I was contributing to the delinquency of a minor and things like that. I guess that she didn't realize that I was as young as Stacy. Anyway, at that point we decided to leave, hitch-hiking up north to Lac Labiche where my grandmother lived. We stayed there two days, went to a party in a small town called Plomondon, then went further north to Fort MacMurray. We kicked around there for a few days and I met this guy named Raymond Bellcourt who took us in his car to these little towns in the area. This was about 250 miles north of Edmonton.

Then one morning about 6 a.m. we started hitch-hiking back to Edmonton after two weeks of small-town life in northern Alberta. About halfway there we got caught in a blizzard. We had been dropped off by the side of the road near a small town and both of us were pretty scared for a while. I'd never been in a prairie blizzard before ... or any kind of blizzard for that matter. Anyway, we managed to get a ride in a truck after an hour or so and reached Edmonton late that night. The next morning I phoned mom and told her we'd decided to go on to Toronto. I had her wire the money I'd saved to the CN Telecommunications office.

It took us six days to get to Toronto hitch-hiking. We didn't have any trouble, except for one night we couldn't get a ride and had to sleep in the lobby of some dumpy hotel in Hoite River. My money was going to Toronto and we didn't have enough to spare for a room. It was the first week in January when we arrived in Toronto.

We got a room in this real creepy boarding house on 83rd

and Spadina Road. There were ten or twelve rooms and about forty hippies living there. Everybody called it a pusher's house. It was really rough and rowdy. Some of the kids were fourteen and fifteen years old or even less. The place was always being raided by the cops. The first time, after Stacy and I had just moved in, we heard this pounding on the door at around 8 p.m.: "Open up, it's the police! This is a raid!" Before I could get to the door some huge cop just knocked it off its hinges on to the floor. Anyway, we just stood there looking at them. Downstairs the younger kids were going out the window across to a house on 84th Street. The cops on this "Morality Squad" ran in and started roaring all over the house, looking everywhere for drugs and stuff that was stolen. Then they checked everyone's ID and showed us pictures of some guys, saying, "Do you know this person?" We'd say "No," without even looking at the pictures. "Look at the picture, punk, and don't get smart!" Then they'd push your face into the picture and make you look at it. "No, no, I've never seen him before." They'd just say, "Yeah, yeah, we know." Finally they left after searching the whole house with flashlights. Whenever they came in, all the electricity was turned off or the bulbs busted.

Sometimes they took someone to the station for questioning or charged them with something. They'd go over to the big house on 84th, but it was owned by this rich woman who wouldn't let them in without a search warrant. She had a lawyer and some pull in town so they couldn't push her too hard. A lot of people, different people, stayed at her place from time to time. It was a huge house.

When the pigs came back that first night after talking to this white woman, they went down in the basement rooms for a closer check. I went upstairs to my room but a guy stopped me and asked me if I wanted to see his new stereo

— which he'd just stolen. I said , "Okay," and we went into his room. We were sitting there not doing anything, when we hear the cops again: "Open up! It's a raid!" We know what's going to happen, so we just sit there. They kicked in the door and roar all over the place looking for stuff. The guy jammed his stereo under the bed and for some reason the cops didn't find it; maybe it was too obvious, or they were in too much of a hurry. Anyway, they left and went into some other rooms.

It was about 4:30 in the morning when they finally left. These raids by the "Morality Squad" became so frequent while I was living at this place that we always tried to stay out till five or so in the morning and sleep during the day. It was a strange world.

Once at around five o'clock in the morning, after I'd just gotten to bed, the cops came and banged and kicked down the door. It was this "Mr. Death's" squad, headed by a well known drug cop named Abe Sedanko. Everyone said, "Oh, it's you. Hello Abraham." He found a roach in one of the ashtrays and really started ripping the place up looking for drugs — tearing up mattresses, breaking in walls, and so on. This guy named Doug came in and asked, "What's wrong Abraham? Why're you getting so excited? Don't get hysteri-cal, okay?" I started going around with this Doug a while before the cops were really harassing him and another guy named John. Just as Doug was saying that Abe wouldn't find any stuff in the place some cop touched a faulty wire and shorted all the lights. Abe panics, whips out his gun, holding a flashlight in Doug's eyes, yells, "Who turned out those damn lights?" "One of your men did, Sir," Doug replied politely. "They hit a faulty wire." Everyone started laughing and Abe just fumbled around, still nervous. His gun still out, he lines us all up against the wall and comes on with this tough talk. The cops start searching us and roughing us up a bit. They got the lights back on, but then Abe shorted the wire again. He was really upset, yelling and waving his gun around. Doug said to him, "Okay, take it easy; and stop pointing that gun at us."

The police were a little edgy because a few weeks earlier this guy Karl Lecours had been shot and killed. It's a long story, but anyway, this Lecours was selling dope to young kids and when one of them, who was about fifteen, refused to pay, Lecours beat him up pretty badly and threatened him with a gun if he didn't pay up. Doug and I were talking about it with this kid, Allen, and his sixteen-year-old brother Mike in their room at the Spadina house. Then, all of a sudden Mike brings out a 303 rifle and shows us a cross he'd cut in the floor. "When Lecours comes for his money I'm going to blow his head off!" Doug was a pretty good friend of Karl's but he thought Mike was only kidding or bluffing; he was sixteen but looked even younger.

Well later, when we were in our own room, we heard this tremendous "boom!" At the same time a bullet tears through our wall, just misses this East Indian's head and finally lodges in a brick wall outside the apartment house. I couldn't believe it: "What's going on here?" I thought. "What's happening?" I was groping around like this when Karl walks in and says, "I thought you were my friend, Doug. I thought you were a friend." Doug told him to shut up, stop talking, but Karl kept repeating that he thought Doug was his friend. His jacket and shirt was bloodsoaked and he walked, or stumbled, around the balcony, down the stairs, then tried to crawl back up. Doug stayed with him and I trailed behind. Finally, Karl fell down. Doug opened his shirt and looked at his chest. It was a real mess. "Just calm down, Karl," Doug said, "You're in bad shape. If you don't quit talking, people will think I have something to do with it. You know I didn't, Karl, so just stop talking."

I just took off after seeing all that blood on Karl's chest. It was too ugly and horrible: Karl bleeding to death and Doug sitting there crying and telling him to shut up.

Anyway, after that they threw everyone in jail who was within a block of the place and then there was a long court case. When the neighbours phoned the police they came and found Doug still crying over the body. "Okay nigger," they said, "let's go! We're charging you with murder!" This Michael kid kept saying, "But I did it! I did it! Don't blame Doug!" At first nobody believed him 'cause he looked so young and innocent. But eventually they did. His kid brother Allen was a real mess; thought the whole thing was a big joke. Luckily, after I'd left the apartment, and just before Lecours died, he said, "Okay Doug. It's okay. I know it wasn't you." A few people heard him and testified to clear Doug. Later this Mike got off too — I think it was because of Karl being a pusher and beating up on Allen to get his money.

There was a lot of violence and death in that place. Once this guy next to me in a restaurant just upped and died of a heart attack. No one even seemed to care; it was just a nuisance. Then there was a lot of open violence by these motorcycle fanatics, and the rough stuff got worse in the higher brackets of the drug scene, where tens and thousands of dollars and more were involved. This was just the beginning, I think, of heroin coming on to the market in a big way. Before, it was mainly pot and hash. (After I left Toronto, Doug got axed in the back. He was just walking down the street, got hit, turned around and this guy says: "Sorry buddy, wrong guy!" and takes off. I heard that the knifing screwed up Doug's nervous system in some way.)

So violence was becoming an everyday occurrence. There was this guy we knew, Greg, who owed some motorcycle gang $150. He was really a nervous sort and quite a joker. He was a mulatto with real frizzy hair and a good friend of ours. Every time we saw him he'd say this gang was going to get him ... and finally they did too. They beat him up real bad and broke one of his legs. These motorcycle gangs were really rough, but they usually attacked women, mugging them and raping them in gangs. This happened quite a lot. Fortunately, they left me alone because I was Doug's girl. They were actually cowards. Even though Doug had been released, he still had a reputation of probably killing someone — his friend Karl — so the gangs didn't mess with him.

Well, after Karl Lecours was killed in our place, the cops were nervous and waved their guns around a lot. Once they raided the place early in the morning and dragged us down to the station. There was this girl Kathy with us; she was really sick. She had these pornographic pictures of herself taken with some other people at a party — a bunch of pictures they'd taken for kicks at some orgy they'd had. She was showing them around while we were waiting at the station ... just like that. Then some cop noticed and snatched the pictures. "Whose are these?" he asked. And this Kathy, of all people, pops up with, "don't know. We just found them here on the bench." It was a joke. The girl in the pictures was Kathy and there was no mistake about it — platinum blond hair and all. The stupid cop looked at the pictures, then at Kathy, then back at the pictures. Finally, he just shook his head, put the pictures in his pocket and walked away.

Then they took us down to the copshop and strip-frisked us. It was my first time and I was a bit scared but this Kathy went berserk and really raised shit. They frisked me first —

two huge police women — then turned to Kathy. We had taken all our clothes off and the made us spread our legs apart and then started probing around everywhere looking for dope. Kathy resisted and started screaming at these police women: "Get your filthy hands off me, you bitch! I'm no queer! But I bet this is really great fun for you — you're just a perverted bitch!" They started slapping her around and she fought back. "Ain't no queer cop's gonna stick their fingers in me or push me around!" Then they really beat her up. It went on for about fifteen minutes but she just wouldn't shut up about these cops being queers and bitches. Finally, they got done with her and let us both go ... just said: "You're clean. Go home!" It was quite an experience.

My sister had been writing us at the Spadina place asking when we were coming home. Stacy wanted to leave Spadina and find another place to live. She was scared after the Lecours shooting and didn't want any trouble with the police. I decided to stay, so a few days later she borrowed some money and clothes saying she wanted to go over and see what Detroit was like. It was about two months before I heard from her again.

Most of the people in the Spadina apartment house were small pushers ... except for the real young kids. There were about ten big dealers who worked the neighbourhood. They worked out of shabby old places — just dirty shacks — but kept fancy apartments in the better parts of town under different names. They lived in these apartments during the day and usually spent all their nights selling stuff out of their joints or at Webster's, which was open till 5 a.m. We'd usually go there around ten or midnight and stay till the early hours of the morning. It was a great hangout for prostitutes, pimps, pushers, perverts and all kinds of creeps — every type and description. This Johnny Webster "owned" the place but told us it was financed by the Mafia — which wasn't hard to believe.

I met a lot of people at Webster's. We'd often just sit there for hours over a cup of coffee. There was this writer friend of Doug's, Jim Cody or something, who worked for a small daily newspaper. He had a friend named Vern who took a liking to me and often gave me some hash or grass. He was a pusher but he didn't charge me anything — not even for the occasional shot of heroin. Some straight people came to Webster's too, either to watch the action or just by mistake. At times the place was a bore and at other times there was a lot of action.

There was this friend of Webster's named Dominique: a big black guy who'd deserted the US Army and crossed into Canada. Once these white guys came in and decided to pick a fight with him — I never found out why. Doug said it was because they wanted to get him in trouble with the police and extradited. Well, they jumped him — six of them — and it was quite a fight. Dominique was strong as a bull, real tough. He took a lot of punishment himself but clearly came out on top. He took this one guy and slid him down the counter, his head crashing into the cash register. When another guy went for the phone, Dominique picked up a meat cleaver and threatened to chop off his hand if he touched it. The fight lasted over half an hour and this Webster never made a move to bring in the cops — which he usually did at the first hint of trouble. He just watched and poured a glass of water on the head of the guy who knocked himself out on the register. "Why don't you be a good fellow and go home?" he said. But the stupid ass still wanted to fight and ended up being thrown out the window.

When it was all over the place was a real mess; seats

smashed, windows broken and so forth. I stayed around to watch most of the fight — just out of curiosity. Then we came back when it was over. This Dominique must have been in with the big boys; he was always flashing a big wad of bills. I think he was a pimp or something. Anyway, when we walked in he was handing Webster a thousand dollars in small bills and telling him: "Ah, Johnny, a good evening's fun, eh? Get your place fixed up with this and let's forget about it." "Sure thing," said Webster, and the next night the place was good as new.

Seemed that everybody I met or knew was into something or running away from something ... or usually both. Ed had run away from Vancouver; Doug had been in on a charge of contributing to the delinquency of a minor and so on. At first I thought it was all kicks; I was still just seventeen and it seemed like a lot of fun and excitement. Like the first time I stayed at Webster's all night — just after I started going with Doug. It was a very cold wintery night in Toronto; it was March already but unlike Vancouver it was still snowing and freezing. The streets were clean and empty, covered with snow. We ran around playing tag and so forth for over an hour, all the way home. It was great fun and I even worked up a sweat in that terrible weather.

The newness and most of the kicks wore out after a month or so. They closed the Spadina house and Doug and I didn't have any place to stay. Doug had been out of work for a while and I never brought in any money. I'd long since spent what I brought with me. For a week or two we moved into Turk Ahmed's place; a real fancy house up on North Spadina. Then we stayed for a week with this Pakistani and finally wound up living in a deserted basement. Doug was really a fine guitarist and singer. He'd had fifteen years of lessons and experience and even spent some time in university and three years in Mexico. He was usually able to earn a good living but for some reason was finding it difficult to get a new job.

Then I just happened to run into Stacy on the street one day. She was dressed up pretty fancy and said, "Hey, Bobbi! I've been looking for you!" She'd been back a couple of weeks from Detroit where she'd become a hooker. She was still working at it when we met. It was really something — the change that had come over her. Real weird. Here was this nice little girl from a small town near Edmonton and the next thing you knew she was a hooker. Christ, I didn't know what was going on. She gave me some money and asked Doug and me to move in with her ... said she'd just rented a nice big place. I told her she didn't have to bother about me but she insisted, saying she wanted to pay me back for all I'd done for her in Vancouver — the money and clothes I gave her before she went to Detroit.

Well, being that we were temporarily desperate, we moved in with her. It wasn't too bad for a while, but after a few weeks it got pretty sick. She was getting really raw, with different guys in all the time and always trying to hustle other girls' boyfriends. Once she said, "You know, Bobbi, I like Doug. Why don't we share him?" And she was very serious. "Fuck it," I told her. "Not that I love him or anything, but if you want him, go ask him yourself!" She never asked him and it didn't go beyond that.

Toronto: Anti-War Demonstrations and Racism

Going around with Doug brought me into contact for the first time with politics, though I was marginal. There were these peace demonstrations and once they got started it seemed we were always going to them. It was funny. They were usually organized by these Trotskyists who would come into the "Village" looking for Doug. They'd usually find him at Webster's and ask him to come along and play his guitar at the rally. The first time this guy comes in and says, "Hey Doug, want to come on this anti-war march?" And Doug says, "Sure, you got an axe?" The guy didn't know what he was talking about, and neither did I. "Axe?" he says. "Sure, eh, no — what the hell's an axe?" "You know," says Doug, "a guitar." "Oh yeah," the guy says, relieved. "Let's go." I didn't care about going, one way or another. By this time I was really passive — sort of subdued. I didn't object to anything and rarely got upset. Doug asked me to come along so I did. It was just after we'd met and I didn't even know he played guitar. I thought he must be some amateur and thought, "Boy, this is all I need."

Then he started playing these marching songs that he sort of made up as he went. People at Webster's came around the table and started asking stupid questions like, "Say, is that a new axe? Where'd you get it?" and so on. Then this kid who couldn't have been over fourteen comes over with a recorder and starts playing along with Doug. I couldn't believe how good he was — and just a kid. The way he played that little recorder made it sound like a saxophone. In a while they got up from the table, left Webster's and started walking around the "Village" — an area maybe a mile square bounded by four main streets: Spadina, Yonge, Wellesley and Bloor. The Village had a reputation as a hangout for motorcycle gangs, hippies, drug pushers, hookers and so forth. Anyway, they started playing and singing this nice song inviting people out to the anti-war demonstration. Doug sang loud and clear and soon a big crowd was following us ... mainly to hear the music. Some Trotskyists were handing out leaflets. People would say, "Oh, yeah, very nice," then throw them away a few minutes later. We went around the Village twice, then headed down Spadina Avenue. It was really funny; people coming out of their houses and following Doug and the music like he was the Pied Piper.

When we reached Queen's Park, a teach-in was going on. Dominique Garcia was there, very excited because he'd managed to organize a Black contingent. Dominique was a Black who'd come over from the Dominican Republic when he was seven. He'd been very active during the American intervention in Santo Domingo — sympathetic to the people's struggle there — and was also working with the local Draft Resisters' and Deserters' Committee of people mainly up from the States. It was a pretty strong organization.

Well, this Dominique waved us up front and asked us to get on the platform and sing. The crowd, about three or four thousand people, contained a lot of East Indians and hippies. There were also some Communists and Trotskyists as well as fifty or so Canadian Nazis shouting their anti-communist, racist crap. Toronto is really quite a fascist town; a lot of reactionary politics tied in with Nazi-type racism against East Indians, Blacks, Native Americans and so on.

Anyway, about a dozen of us got up on this wooden platform and Doug had his guitar. I was just sitting on the edge of the platform, looking out over the crowd, not doing very much. They were playing and singing these anti-war songs and the fascists didn't like it at all. They were screaming: "Get those niggers off the stage!" The crowd shouted back: "Shut up! Let them sing!" It wasn't long before the Communists and Nazis were fighting. We just kept singing, louder, while they were yelling and fighting. Soon you couldn't hear a thing — just a blur of noise. It was really quite a teach-in. Well, the police came along in about ten minutes, riding their big horses through the crowd and over to where the trouble was. They broke up the fight, rounded up the Trots and Communists but didn't touch the fascists!

This rally was really something new for me. Before, I didn't even know there were fascists or Nazis in Canada. When the big fight broke out, one of the Nazis grabbed my leg and tried to pull me down off the platform. I kicked the guy in the face with my free foot and jumped up on the stage. It was strange. I was just standing there and the crowd was applauding, clapping for me. Doug challenged the guy to come up on the stage with him but he refused. They were cowards when they had to fight one at a time. But groups of them were out in the crowd kicking and beating hippies.

Well, when the police came people started shouting, "Back to the Consulate! Back to the Consulate!" At first they shouted it, then it became a chant and finally a song. Most of the crowd fell in behind and started marching off to the U.S. Consulate, with the fascists and the police harassing them all the way. I stayed behind for a while, just sitting and thinking. I didn't understand much of what had gone on, but I knew I didn't like the fascists at all. They were anti-Indian, anti-communist, anti-everything that wasn't white and patriotic. "Why did they even come, the noisy bastards?" I thought. It was just a hippie kind of analysis — because that's where I was at: "You do your thing and let me do mine! I mind my business, you mind yours! The U.S. has no business in Vietnam, so they should get out and let the Vietnamese do their own thing!"

We went to a lot of demonstrations after this one, but it was a good introduction. After the march on the Consulate about six hundred people came back for the teach-in. The Trotskyists had rented the platform so the cops couldn't very well chase them off. When the cops were charging and there was a lot of fighting it was real exciting for me. But when these draft resisters and deserters started talking, my mind kept wandering; I just couldn't listen. I looked around at the crowd and wondered why I was even there.

You see, I was really just an appendage of Doug. He had an interest in politics but I was just there for the kicks. After the teach-in a bunch of us went some place to eat. Doug was babbling on about the draft resisters' movement, whether it was really political. When someone asked him if he was a draft resister, Doug said "No. I'm 4-F." The guy asked him how he'd managed it and Doug told him that when he was nineteen he had rickets and when he went for his army physical in Harlem he'd been on junk for a while and wasn't eating — had lost a lot of weight. Well, they tested him, found the rickets and gave him a 4-F. After that he spent about three months in the hospital; they'd pulled him in as a junkie. Then he came up to Canada and stayed off drugs. He started playing the guitar seriously, singing and travelling around. He was even in Vancouver for a while. I never met him but did hear him sing in a hippie joint on 4th Avenue. Then in Toronto some guy asked if he would help them in the draft resister's organization. So he did. He went to these meetings every Saturday, sang at rallies, helped draft resisters find places to stay and so forth. He also belonged to some Afro-Canadian Society. In about 1971, long after I'd left Toronto, they started putting out this paper called the Black Liberation News. It was mostly about struggles by Blacks going on in Africa, the Dominican Republic and, to some extent, in Canada — though there wasn't much happening here.

My interest in politics was mainly because of all the hassles and racist crap we had to take from the cops. They'd always address you by using some racist label. Black people they called "niggers," Italians were "wops" and Indians were always "squaws" or "redskins." They had these little class and racists slots they'd put you into and were pretty brutal — pushing and shoving everyone around.

Then there was another thing which turned me off to the system. I tried to apply for welfare and really got worked over by the bureaucracy. At first they told me I had to prove I wasn't a Registered Indian. "How can I prove that?" I asked. "Maybe I can prove what I am, but how can I prove what I am not?" But that's the way it was. So then I go over to the Indian Affairs Bureau and they ask me to prove I was registered. Well, I thought it would be easy, but being a Métis from B.C. with no papers they just refused to believe me. So that was that: no welfare from the city because I couldn't prove I wasn't a Registered Indian, and no assistance from Indian Affairs because I couldn't prove I was a Registered Indian.

Maybe, if I'd have pursued the thing higher up in the

bureaucracy I could have gotten something. But I was really ashamed and the whole thing seemed such an ugly mess. "Fuck it!" I thought. "I'm not going begging any more." Like I mentioned before, my mom was always proud of never having asked for welfare, even though she really needed it at times, and it was the same for her whole family. They had been broke and sick but mom was real proud they never once asked for welfare. With us kids she would always say it was shameful to be a welfare recipient. She'd even whisper when she said the word, like it was poison. Well, you can see how I was ashamed even before I applied. It was only that Doug told me to, saying "Why not, the money's there, why don't you take it? Nothing to be ashamed of." But it was really traumatic when they turned me down; I finally went begging for money and they wouldn't give it to me!

The racism thing came up again when Doug and I were trying to rent a place. We brought this white guy along figuring it would be easier, but they would just say "Yes" to the white guy and me and "no" to Doug ... Right in front of him they'd say, "You two are alright, but not him." This happened several times. I was bugged by it and Doug was furious. He took it to some agency which was supposed to investigate charges of discrimination, but nothing ever came of it. When asked, the owners would just say they turned us down because they didn't rent three to a room. I didn't even want to go on looking. That had never happened to me in Vancouver; they'd always say the place was taken or filled up, not straight out that they didn't want you because you were an Indian.

Whenever we got turned down, Doug would almost boil over with anger. He was a big guy: about 6 feet 2 inches and 200 pounds. His hands were huge and he'd taken a lot of karate. When he got angry he'd point this long finger at you.

Once when this puny little manager turned us down Doug started talking very slowly and quietly, but then gradually his voice got louder and louder as he stood pointing his finger at this guy. The fellow got so scared he peed his pants. He was shivering all over saying, "I'm just the caretaker. I don't make the policies. Please don't hit me, don't hit me!" We left him there crying with his wet pants. I found it really funny and laughed about it for the next two weeks. "There was one bloody landlord that got close to what was coming to him," I thought.

Most of the time these landlords and managers just ran into their rooms when Doug started to get angry. Sometimes they'd call the police. Doug never hit anyone but when he got mad it always seemed like he was about to kill them. His white friend kept telling him, "Calm down Doug, calm down. Remember, that hand of yours is a lethal weapon. You'll get five years if you hit him." And it was true; if you hit someone and knew a certain amount of karate or boxing you could get charged with assault with a deadly weapon … a five-year rap.

"A Real Bad Trip"

Most of the time in Toronto I had these feelings of being useless. Like I never thought much about any particular situation I was in, just about the uselessness of my existence. I felt like a bump on a log and then would get this feeling that I wanted to at least be a "mobile" bump — to control my existence a little and do something useful, I'd remember when my grandfather was looking after me and would always say: "Whatever you do, be useful, because life is full of people who just exist and are empty." I grew up agreeing with this philosophy — that most people were useless and that it was important to do something useful. My mom was the same way; she was always worrying about just being a mother and living from day to day ... just existing. I used to think that there had to be something I could do to leave my mark, to be useful to other people. I'd tried working, but most of my jobs were of the "shit work" variety and I didn't find them meaningful. Like when I was younger, baby-sitting, or doing this selling on the phone. Every afternoon when school was out I'd go home and try to sell people something over the phone so I could get a bonus. I was only fourteen but even then started thinking that this working business was pretty useless — just an empty existence. I kept that phoning job for a few months, then quit.

In Toronto, Doug used to get on me about getting a job. But he was the same as me: didn't want to just work for money, doing empty work. He liked playing guitar but he couldn't always get playing and singing jobs. He'd trained at university to do accounting and sometimes he'd look for that kind of job when he was between singing engagements. He hated the work but would really get mad when they turned him down because he was Black. These employment agencies would usually tell him: "It's not very likely we'll be able to get you a job." Then they'd call a potential employer and tell him they had this "coloured accountant." When Doug heard this he really blew his stack. He'd say something like, "I'm not asking you to sell my colour, man — just my skill! Get it!"

Anyway, Doug was always trying to get me to find a job, support myself and move out of the village. He finally moved out, but that was after we split up. He moved in with his sister, who had a pretty nice little house just outside the city. She was a CBC script assistant and had a kid. After that, Doug came to visit me once in a while and still kept saying I should move out of the village and get a job. This Turk Ahmed was also trying to get me to smarten up but I just couldn't see any reason for working, for just putting in time. I didn't want a life of work, home, TV; work, home, TV. I'd lived like that before and hated every minute of it. So I just didn't do anything.

My relationship with Doug was kind of strange; it was never a reciprocal relationship. Doug would always try to get me to talk with him, to form some kind of deep relationship, but I'd just cut him off, or cut myself off, at a certain point. If I didn't want to talk, I didn't talk. And if Doug was talking about something I didn't want to hear, I didn't listen. It was weird. I was an appendage — kind of a parasite — but at the same time I was detached and unconcerned.

It was like with this guy Nat, who was sort of a local nut. Doug and I were fairly close friends with Jamaican George, a Cree/Jamaican half-breed from some reservation. He was a little guy who looked just like an Indian except that he was much darker. He was pretty black, in fact, and I remember it striking me funny that he could speak fluent Cree. I could remember hearing a lot of Cree from the time I was a young kid but I couldn't speak it. Jamaican George taught me a few songs in Cree after a while and we'd sing them together while Doug played guitar. Anyway, this Nat was trying to split me and Doug up for some reason. He'd make up all these stories about Doug and George, how they were always talking about me behind my back, asking nasty things, telling lies about me and so forth. Well, you'd think I'd get real mad or something, but I just thought Nat was nutty. And besides, I didn't really care. I'd just say, "That's okay, so what? If that's their shallow thing, let them do it."

As it turned out, this Nat was doing the same thing with Jamaican George, telling him that Doug and I were making fun of him behind his back. And he was doing it with Doug too — telling him what George and I were saying about him. Finally, he talked himself into a corner and we all began to wonder what was going on. George started it by asking Doug and I what we thought Nat's game was. (In Toronto everything was a "game," and everybody had one.) I said, "I don't know. Why?" So he starts telling us what Nat said about us talking about him and then it all came out. Later Nat came in, sitting down and acting all friendly. We just stared at him real cold for about five minutes until he got the idea and left. I never saw him again in Toronto.

The point, though, was that I really didn't care. And what was worse — what I hated the most — was that I had kind of lost all sense of emotion. I remember even when Karl Lecours was lying there in his own blood. I just stared at him. Doug was taking off his shirt and crying like a baby, but I was just staring at him wondering if I should react in some way, do something. Here was this guy shot and bleeding to death, Doug crying and all upset and me thinking: "Maybe there's some way I should be reacting to this? Something I should be doing?"

This kind of deadening of emotion in me began when I was about thirteen and really started hating school. I had some confidence in my ability to think, but the longer I stayed in school, wrote their stupid essays, listened to their stupid crap and so on, the less I was able to figure out what was going on around me — especially at home where the emotional climate was really awful. My old lady was always nagging my dad and he'd have these long sullen periods and then blow up and go rank on everybody; then he'd become sullen again, mom would start nagging and telling him he should leave and sometimes he did. This was happening all the time so there was always this tense, really tense, atmosphere around the house. I just slowly lost my ability to understand it or live with it emotionally. So I started cutting myself off, just accepting it and after a while being bored with it. At the same time, I started getting less and less interested in people and their problems — I didn't want to get involved. Things at home seemed to be getting worse but I was getting less concerned about it. My sisters were always being hassled by my mom and forbidden to do the things I had done. They weren't allowed out past ten o'clock and stuff like that. And when they were sixteen they didn't have a chance to learn to drive and get a license like I did. It seemed strange and unfair but at the same time I was getting less concerned about it. I'd just think: "It's not my problem to worry about what's happening with other people, what they're doing. I just have to be concerned with me, control my own existence."

But then in Toronto I started to lose control of my existence and that's what really demoralized me. Here I was, living this completely useless life, thinking about it, but not able to do anything about it, to get out of it. And it was hard to tell if I really cared — about anything. Like with Doug. I never got angry at him; I wasn't that emotionally involved to get angry. I liked him. He was an alright guy. If I had to live with someone it might as well be him. But he liked me a lot; it was different with him — he cared, was emotionally involved with me.

It was sometime in May 1968 when my brother Ed came back from Vancouver. My mother had sent him to bring me home. I remember we were at this small party with a bunch of Jamaicans, Indians and a couple of Italians and Jewish guys — Doug had this wide circle of friends, all different types. Anyway, we were there telling jokes and singing songs that were peculiar to our particular cultures. I knew only one Cree song well enough to sing and was embarrassed when I sang it. Not because I didn't like the song or was ashamed of it but because I was such a lousy singer. You see, to be a Cree singer traditionally required years of training — especially the lead singer, who sang the first round with others coming in like an echo. So there was real status to being a Cree singer and I couldn't do any justice to it at all — wasn't even a full Cree and didn't speak more than a few words of the language.

Well, anyway, all of a sudden a rock hit the window of this dumpy little place we were in. I looked out and it was Ed. He'd written me about his conversion after returning to Vancouver and I thought, "Oh, no, this is all I need; my moralistic, idiot brother." He'd gotten all this Christian morality about marriage, "nice" girls and all that crap. I had a feeling I knew what would happen. But when Ed came in and saw Doug they started hugging and carrying on. They'd known each other before but hadn't been real good friends. It didn't matter, though, because Doug was a gregarious guy who hugged and kissed everyone. I was sort of taken aback. Ed wasn't ordinarily very emotional or demonstrative; he just seemed to get caught up in the mood of the party. People were drinking this very strong Jamaican rum — which was illegal to import at that time. Everybody except Doug was pretty well thrashed on just a few sips. Doug didn't drink much and was always careful about not getting drunk and losing his capacity to think and act. He was just that sort of person.

I was pretty drunk by the time Ed arrived ... drunk but not sloppy. I never got sloppy when I drank. I just sat around and laughed when something was funny, going along with the mood of the crowd ... if they were getting angry, so would I. It was a good way to be — never sloppy or conspicuous, always blending in with the crowd.

Anyway, nothing happened that night, but the next day Ed and Doug went out together. I thought, "Oh, no. Doug's sure to tell him we're living together." Well, they had this big argument and came back. Doug was really upset because Ed had made some comment about his being a pimp. The stereotype of a Black man in Toronto is that he is a pimp and Doug always hated that. People would say things behind his back because he always had money. But when he was working he sometimes made $200 a night — and that's a lot of money even if you spend it frivolously like Doug did. Ed just got caught up in the usual racist stereotype and local gossip.

Doug came back first and told me Ed didn't want us living together; that if I didn't come home with him he'd tell my mom and she'd get the police after me. By the time Ed came in I was really angry. "You don't mean anything to me!" I told him. "And the family even less, 3,000 miles away! I don't miss any of you and I'm not homesick. I don't want to go home and I'm not going home! If mom wants to have me put in jail, well, that's just fine. I'll get out!"

I rambled on like that for a time and Ed kept trying to reason with me. After a while all I said was, "Fuck you! Fuck off!" I'd say it again and again, every time he started talking. I wouldn't even hear him out. Then he came on with all this crap about me marrying Doug and I said, "But I don't want to marry Doug! I don't even love him! If he asked me to marry him I'd say "No." Ed was shocked. "Why are you living with him then?" he asked. "Don't you love the guy?" I said, "No! And what difference does it make if I'm living with him?"

Ed was really upset by all this — especially that I didn't even pretend that Doug and I had a serious relationship. He just shook his head and walked out, saying he'd rented a place at 81 Spadina.

By this time I was doing a lot of drugs. There was this guy I mentioned, Vern, who was giving it to me. I had been shooting up heroin for about three months and was getting less and less interested in people generally — in everything. Doug started noticing it after a while. "What's wrong with you?" he'd ask. "Aren't you interested in anything any more?" I wouldn't even answer — just ignore it.

Doug was singing almost everyday, and when he wasn't singing or practicing he'd be down at the gym working out. We spent only a few hours together most days; the rest of the time he was doing his thing and I was doing mine — only he didn't know what I was doing, just assumed I was sitting home watching TV or something. Anyway, by the time I was shooting three or four times a day he found out and told me to leave. He was twenty-five and had talked to me a lot about his own bad experience with dope — what happens to you. He'd say, "Don't even bother trying it because all it'll do is get you into trouble." But I never listened to him; what he said never had any effect on me. Well, when he found out he just couldn't take it. He knew what junkies were like and knew that I'd get that way after a while. "Junkies are dangerous people," he said, "and I don't want to end up supporting your habit! The guy who's giving it to you now will eventually want some bread for it and I'd have to pay. No thanks! If you had a drinking problem ... well, okay. But not junk!" He didn't try to talk me out of it, just said: "It's your decision. You made it and you'll have to live with it, but not me."

So I split with Doug. I think he felt sort of guilty about my doing drugs — maybe a little responsible because I was only seventeen and was living with him. He didn't tell Ed, in any event. I moved in with the guy who'd been giving me the stuff and stayed there a couple of weeks. I felt sort of sad about doing Doug in that way because he really liked me and I had felt very little for him. I just lived with him for convenience sake; it was nice to have a man around and he was the best I could find at the time. This started to really make me feel bad.

Then there was this Vern. He'd been a friend before but now I couldn't stand him. My reasons for staying with him were so sick, so pukey, that I didn't even like to look at him. As soon as I got the fix, I'd want to bugger off and get out of there. Usually I went to the United Church which sort of catered to hippies — they stayed open in the evenings, served coffee and doughnuts, and so on. They had a few chess boards around on tables and I learned to play just to pass the time. I got fairly good after a while and sometimes the people I played with bought me a meal. Most of the time I didn't have any money.

I'd started shooting just once in a while, for kicks. Then it was once a day, twice a day, and so on. I just about overdosed a few times but I could really take a lot. I think that unconsciously I wanted to overdose; I really hated my existence. I had taken this path deliberately, not out of ignorance or naïveté, and was just giving up on life. I knew the stuff would eventually kill me, yet I kept on taking it. And in the meantime I started feeling completely dehumanized, like a vegetable. I actually stopped acting like a human being — didn't laugh, didn't cry, didn't find things funny or sad.

It hit me when this guy I was talking to just dropped dead in the street. We'd had lunch together and I knew him fairly well. Then he drops dead and I say, "What a bummer." I knew I wasn't given to outpourings of emotion but never realized it had gotten so bad that I could just pass off someone's life without a flicker of feeling. It should have at least been a shock, but it wasn't. I just didn't care; it was just a bother. I simply wasn't interested in people any more ... and this worried me. I'd even stopped going to this coffee house hangout because the people bored me; everything bored me.

Vern was a big pusher and real sick ... I mean with people. He was rich enough to support the habit for a few friends, who would become dependent on him — and he really liked that. There was this Bill Cody who wasn't making much money but was really wired to the stuff. He would come and beg Vern to give him a fix and Vern loved it. He didn't use the stuff much himself, just once in a while, being careful not to get addicted to it. But he liked to see other people get strung out on it. At first I didn't realize how sick the guy was; maybe because I never wanted it so bad. I could feel the depression coming on and generally handled it quite well. At first, you see, it's not a physical ache or pain you feel when you start to come down; it's just a feeling of depression. But with this Cody guy it was real physical pain because he'd been on the stuff for over two years. He'd just go ape, crawling around and begging: "Please Vern, please. I gotta have a fix! Please, please!"

Well, I never got this bad and didn't beg. But I was starting to weaken and really began hating the come-down depressions. Then there were a couple of times when I came real close to begging. I would be wishing like hell that I could do up but I'd say to myself, "Just take it easy! If you don't get it, you don't get it. Let's not get caught up in that begging routine!" When I saw these other friends begging, I wasn't bothered at all … at least until I came close to it myself. As I said, after you've been doing smack for a while you just lose any sense of emotion; you get completely dehumanized and don't feel anything for anybody. So when this Cody guy or some other friend would come begging, I wasn't concerned. It's really fantastic what that stuff does to you! I knew intellectually that in other circumstances a scene like that would have bothered me (I'd always been a bit sensitive to other people), but at that time I felt nothing, nil, except maybe a little irritated at the guy for doing it, for not having more control over himself. "If you can't get it, you can't get it!" I thought. "Why plead with that idiot?"

It got to the point where this Vern just made my skin crawl. I couldn't stand having him touch me anymore and started thinking I had to get off the stuff and away from him. But it wasn't easy. You've got to understand that this was a period in my life when I began to see or understand a lot with my mind, but my body wouldn't do anything about it. It was mainly the dope. I knew I would be doing something else, something different, but I just couldn't. Fortunately, I never completely lost hope that there was some way to change all this shit around, to somehow be able to get on top of things, see the whole picture, then say, "This is the way it is; this is what I should be doing!" and then do it. I knew there was something wrong about the whole bloody system, but there were huge gaps in my knowledge. Sometimes I'd ask Doug and other people, "How is this whole fucking economy run?" I learned a little from Doug, and a couple of liberals who speculated on land told me that Americans controlled the Canadian economy. So I started thinking about this: "Who actually owns and controls things?" "But who owns these apartments? Where is all the money going? Not to the bloody managers; they're just working there. It must be someone else. But who? Who owns it all?" I kept asking myself these questions, but it was a long time before I got any answer that made sense.

I was also hung up on what I guess you'd call individualism. Anyway, I always thought I had to solve something in my own mind before I could do anything about it ... and this made it difficult for me to accept anything Doug or some of the other people I knew said. My whole family was like that. My mother always told us: "You have to think for yourselves!" When I was six years old, I asked if I could go to the store and she just said, "You'll have to decide for yourself. Someday I may not be around and you'll have to be able to figure out on your own what to do." So instead of asking people a lot of questions and accepting what I heard, I kept trying to figure things out for myself.

But the more I got into drugs the less I bothered to think

about political or economic things. I started thinking more and more that maybe this was my last stop. "Is this the end of the line for me?" I'd think. I used to make a lot of analogies — like seeing my life like a train and saying to myself: "You're either riding it or you're off; either you lead a useful productive life or you get off somewhere, lay by the wayside and never get going again. Maybe Toronto is the end of the line for me; maybe someday I'll just drop dead on the sidewalk, be buried in some cemetery and that would be it? Simple. And nobody would miss me! Oh, yeah, mom would cry — but that would be it. I wouldn't even have left a small fingerprint, made the slightest dent; my life wouldn't have counted for anything, I'd just be gone." I thought like this a lot, believing this might be the end for me but not wanting it to be so. But what could I do? I didn't want to get some stupid job and make that the end of the line — start working and stop living. I could go back to school, but that was no different than working — just as mechanical and demoralizing. So I just did nothing, except take drugs, for what seemed a very long time ... but even then I'd be thinking that there must be another way.

Well, one morning I decided that was it — I had to get out! So I packed my suitcase and took it over to Ed's place. At least I'd get away from Vern. But then I went and got really spaced out on dope. I shot heroin and also took some crystal methedrine and it felt like I was being torn and pulled in two entirely different directions. Usually I didn't run around or talk with people a lot when I was doing speed. I tried to keep it under control so that I looked fairly normal even when I was high on the stuff. I'd try to think about things, usually just clever little things that I would smile at. That way people never really knew I was doing speed or smack. This time it was different. We were at Cody's place and all of a sudden I bolted out the door and started running like mad down the street. It was real spooky. I couldn't figure out where I was, even though I'd lived in that same area since coming to Toronto. I ran around for a while then jumped on a subway and went all the way out to Abramson where this friend of Doug's lived. Getting off the subway, I suddenly realized how strange it was, me going to this guy's place and all; so I ran like crazy to the other side of the platform — losing my shoes on the way — and took the next subway back.

I decided to go to Ed's place and was charging up Spadina when this guy stopped me and asked where Webster's was. "Oh, it's up that way ... No! It's down that way. Shit! I don't know where it is anymore!" So the guy says, "Maybe you'd better stay with me; you don't look too good." "Fuck you!" I said. "You ask me for directions, then you want me to stay with you!" He was pretty young kid about seventeen. "Look," he said, "you're stoned, I'm just lost!" Then I ran off yelling, "I can't stand it! I can't stand it! I can't stand it!"

I was still yelling when these mulattos up from Detroit stopped me. They thought I was a mulatto too, because they had pretty fair skin, more like Indians than Blacks. Anyway, they stopped me and I piled into their car. I don't know why. They were joking a lot and half drunk on Jamaican rum. When they offered me a drink I took it, thinking it might bring me down a bit. I was flying so bloody high it was unbelievable! And these guys knew it. "Where do you live, honey?" they asked. "Spadina," I answered. The rum hadn't helped at all — I still couldn't remember Ed's address. "But Spadina's a long street, baby. What's the address? The number?" "I used to know it," I said, trying to look like I knew what was going on.

Well, they just kept driving up and down Spadina between the place where it starts and the 100-block. It took two hours, but finally I recognized Ed's building. "Great," they said, "now you just go in and cool down." So I went in, hardly conscious that I'd lost my shoes. I straightened up a bit when I saw Ed. He was the kind of person who'd have turned me in if he knew I was stoned. I just walked in, grabbed my suitcase and started back out the door. "Where you going already? You just moved in," he said. "Oh, I'm going to stay at Stacy's?" She didn't live too far from Ed. "Are you sure you're going to Stacy's?" he asked. I said, "No Ed, I'm going home." "Good," he said. "Are you sure you can make it?" "Oh yeah," I said, "It's okay."

I was kind of surprised that Ed didn't say, "Well, why don't I take you home?" But he didn't. I asked him for a quarter for the subway and he handed it to me. I went out with my suitcase and started running around looking for Stacy to say goodbye. Than all of a sudden this hand reached out and grabbed me. I froze, dropped my suitcase and turned around. It was Doug. "Where are you going in such a hurry?" he asked. "Home," I said. "Well, I'll write and send for you some day when you've got things straightened out."

"Sure," I said, "that's fine. You write me." I knew he'd never write and that I'd never be going back to Toronto.

Anyway, he walked me to the subway and I caught one headed out of town. At the end of the line I got out and started walking west on the highway. It was mid-June 1968 and I was heading home ... if I could make it. I took my last couple of caps of dope along, thinking I might need them on the road. They were gone before I even got out of Toronto. But anyway, I was on my way home after a real bad trip.

Involved With
Life Again

It was really tough hitch-hiking back to Vancouver. At first, I thought I was losing my marbles. I had these hallucinations or something, dreaming that my sister was there and we were talking ... yet being wide awake and fully aware that it wasn't really happening, that it was a dream. I was in the cab of a truck, trying not to say anything out loud and thinking somewhere in the back of my head that if these truckers knew I was flipped out on drugs they might do anything. "These guys are really down on drugs," I thought. "They might even pitch me out without stopping the truck!"

So I managed to keep my mouth shut and after a while started thinking about what had happened to me in Toronto, about my life in that ugly city. Then I said to myself, "You should do this rethinking without the dreaming business!" So finally the dreams or hallucinations went away. We'd been driving a half-hour or so and I asked the truck driver to let me off. He pulled over and after they'd gone on I just sat by the roadside. I was getting pretty depressed and upset and there was no predicting what I might do. That's why I had to get away from the truckers. I hadn't had any dope for a few hours and didn't want to be around people while I was coming down. So I just sat and after a time I started walking. I walked on and on, about twenty miles that first day. Then I just about collapsed. I'd lost a lot of weight and strength during my stay in Toronto — was down from 130 to 102 pounds. I'd let myself get into very bad shape —

physically, mentally and emotionally — and must have looked about 35 years old.

While walking I thought about the card I'd gotten back in Toronto saying that my brother Roger was getting married. "Gee," I thought, "I wish I could have been at the wedding." For some reason, I had always wanted to be there the day Roger got married and now I was very sad about having missed it. "I'll go home and see Roger, talk to him!" I thought. I knew he wouldn't give me any sympathy or understanding; he was tough that way. He'd just say, "you chose it, now you regret it, now you know." All I'd get was flack from him, but I wanted to see him anyway.

After I stopped walking, I just laid down beside the road. Sometime later, a half-breed drove by and saw me there. He stopped, thinking I was a drunk Indian woman, and put me in his car. We drove to the ranch where he was foreman. Later, when I woke up in this strange place, I asked him what was going on. He said something to me in Cree and I told him I didn't speak Cree; that I was from Vancouver. He asked if I spoke French and I said "Yes." So we spoke in French from then on. We were in a French community in Manitoba and he knew only a little English. Anyway, he told me how he'd found me and driven me to the ranch; then he asked how I was feeling. I told him I was very tired from hitch-hiking and walking. "You are also very sick," he said, "and you must rest." So he fed me and then I slept the rest of the night on his couch.

In the morning he asked if I wanted to stay until his wife had her baby. She was due any day and he needed some help … or so he said. So I said, "That's fine with me." That same week his wife had the baby. I didn't know she was going to have it at home, and I wasn't really prepared for it. Anyway, I guess I did all right — taking the hot towels and stuff to the doctor and passing it to him as he needed it. I guess I was surprised and a bit pleased that I was able to maintain my cool during the delivery. Anyway, when it was over, I went out, got on one of his horses and just rode around the fields for a while.

His wife had been very good during the whole thing. And it was right at home there; no anaesthesia or anything like that. Just the doctor, and he delivers the baby and leaves — that was it. Next day the wife was up and looking after the kid. She was very young too, about twenty, and they had two other kids already. He was about thirty.

I wanted to leave the next day, so he drove me about 75 miles to the next town — going way out of his way. Soon I got picked up by two woodsmen who drove me about two hundred miles. Then I got a ride to Medicine Hat, Alberta, and from there this old guy took me to the junction going to Nelson, British Columbia. On the way, he bought me some cookies, pop and a chocolate bar and gave me five dollars. Just a nice old guy.

But then I ran into some trouble. And it was a good thing I'd begun to get into better shape and was in a good state of mind, or it might have been much worse. Anyway, these two guys pick me up and while we're driving keep joking around that they're going to rape me and stuff like that. I just said, "Oh yeah, sure" — but I was looking around wondering what I could hit them with. Then I remember that I still have this six-pack of pop with me and think, "Ah, that's it!"

Soon they started talking about raping me more seriously. I said, "You guys are just joking." I had been in the back seat alone but they slowed down and this one guy jumps in the back and starts mauling me — pushing me around and trying to scare me. They said they'd stolen the car, but I said

"Bullshit! It's your car and I've got the license number!" Then I told them the number; fortunately, I still had a good memory for numbers. It was one of the few things I could still do with my mind.

Well, the guy driving starts to pull over and says, "Take her shirt off, Billy!" He grabs my shirt and rips it halfway off before I can push his hand away. Then, practically without thinking, I grab this bottle and whack him over the head real bloody hard; so hard the bottle breaks and he goes down unconscious. We were almost stopped and, pointing the broken bottle at the driver, I leaned over and pulled out the keys, saying. "Your friend got it pretty bad and you're going to die if you try anything!"

The car stopped. The guy I'd hit was moaning and I knew I had to act quickly. But I was still so scatter-brained that I couldn't think straight — partly because I'd gotten hit pretty hard in the eye by this guy while he was trying to tear my shirt off. "Should I leave them here and throw away the keys or have them drive me to the police station in town?" We were just outside a small town named Grand Forks. I was still pointing this bottle at the one guy and wondering out loud, "What should I do with you now?" "Ah, we were just joking," the guy says. "I wasn't serious at all!" "Bullshit!" I said, but I had to act quick; my thinking capacity was wearing real thin — and was already thin to begin with. The tension was getting to me. So wanting more to be away from them than anything else, I threw the keys off into the bush, checked the guy's head to see if he'd make it, and then ran off toward the town.

Grand Forks was only a mile away from the car and I could see it down the hill. I started off carrying my suitcase and the five bottles left in my case of pop. About half-way down, the suitcase got to feeling real heavy, so I just threw it aside. For some strange reason, I kept the case of pop. When I got to the police station I thought, "They'll never believe me — I must look like a real mess! Maybe they'll even think I tried to rob those guys." Anyway, they talked to me for a while, asking were I lived, who my parents were and all that kind of crap. I gave them my brother Roger's phone number and they called him up, asking if I was his sister. Roger said, "Yeah, sure she is! And she's on her way home. She's been touring around the country, hitch-hiking." After the call they believed me and asked if I wanted to lay charges against the two guys. The thought of staying around there to press charges really blew my mind. I said: "No, please, — I just want to get out of here and go home!" They said "Okay" and I went out on the highway and started walking west.

After about three hours, I reached another small town not far from Grand Forks. Then I got a ride from this guy. He kept asking if I'd had any trouble. "Come all the way from Toronto, have you? Sure looks like you've had some trouble." "Oh, no," I said, "no trouble." But he kept insisting that something must have happened and finally I asked him, "Why are you so sure I've been in some trouble?" "Well," he said, "there's blood all over you and your clothes are all torn." I looked down at my hands and they were covered with dried blood. Must have been from when I was examin-ing this guy's head to see how bad he was hurt. I'd never washed it off ... never even noticed it! I'd been smoking, had brushed my hair, but never even noticed all this blood on my hands. It was weird. And my shirt was badly ripped and had blood on it too. The guy must have been affected; anyway, he was real nice — bought me a meal and drove me right to my brother's house in Vancouver.

I thought I knew the house number and street, but when

we got there I wasn't sure. I thanked the guy for the ride and went in. It was around 8 o'clock in the morning. Roger and Donna were there; they just looked at me, then fed me and told me to go to sleep. I slept around the clock, waking up the next morning. Roger finally asked, "Well, what happened to you?" I said, "What do you mean 'what happened'? It was a whole lot of things, not a simple event!"

I just told them a little of what had happened in Toronto … and some lies too. I avoided telling them about me being on heroin; just said I'd been without a place to live for a long time, couldn't find a job and eventually decided to come home. A lot of crap like that. Then Roger asked, "What happened between you and Ed? He went to bring you home." "Ah, it was nothing … just like at home. We had some fights and he took off. I stayed with him for awhile before I left. He's still there I guess." Roger didn't believe my story, but he didn't press me for any more information. It was two years before I told him that I'd been on dope in Toronto.

I was still in pretty rough shape. The first thing I did after my talk with Roger was go downtown to the courthouse where all the hippies used to hang around. I bought some dope from a guy I'd known in Toronto, thinking: "Maybe some grass will straighten me out." But I really needed something by this time. I got stoned and then went with some of the family down to Lynn Valley, where they were having a fair with rides and sports events and so on. I'd been fairly athletic in school and had even won a gold medal in track when I was very young. Now it was a joke. I was in such terrible shape by that time that I didn't think I could walk, let alone run. I'd gone down from 130 to 100 pounds and smoked like a fiend — especially after going off heroin;

seemed I always had to be smoking. Anyway, I entered one short race and won the stupid thing. Then I went into the sack race and was hopping along pretty well before I fell flat on my face. I was bleeding from the forehead and nose, and they dragged me off the field. I wasn't hurt bad and couldn't stop laughing. Then my mom came over, patched me up a bit and said, "You're sure acting awful strange today, Bobbi." I think she knew I was stoned, but she didn't say anything more.

I'd been home about two weeks when mom asked what I was going to do. It was July, 1968, and I'd just had my eighteenth birthday. Toni had written offering me a place to stay and recuperate and mom said, "Maybe you should go down and visit Toni." I wasn't getting along too well at home, so I just said "Okay." I was still in a very depressed and bored state of mind ... at least most of the time. I had started reading a bit, though, which was something I'd almost forgotten how to do. It was real slow going because I hadn't done any reading since I was around thirteen. Even in school I rarely read the textbooks; I would just listen in class and take the exams on the basis of that — which was usually good enough to get me pretty fair marks.

So in a couple of days I took the bus down to Porterville and lived with Toni, Arturo and their kids. I stayed there about two months, sort of drying out. I'd decided before leaving Vancouver to lay off dope for good. Toni was real nice, as usual, but Arturo had become a real fascist. After a while, I didn't see how Toni could go on living with him. He was working in some psychiatric hospital and Toni had developed the typical "white" woman mentality — doing the cooking, cleaning, shopping and taking care of the kids.

All in all, though, I didn't mind staying with them; they were the closest thing to normal that I'd experienced in over six months.

Lorenzo wasn't around — fortunately. He'd been writing to me, to my mom, everybody, saying he was madly in love with me, wanted to marry me and so on. He even said he would come up to Canada to marry me and live here — but I said "No." My mom would say, "Sounds like he really loves you, Bobbi. Why don't you go back and marry him?" I'd reply: "What's love?" — in a really callous way, which kind of upset her. Anyway, Lorenzo had finally been drafted into the army and sent to Vietnam. In his letters he'd say he couldn't stand it — all the bullshit that was going on. The South Vietnamese Army was full of "traitors" always firing on US troops. Lorenzo kind of liked the idea of that, saying, "It serves the Yankees right being fired on by their own puppets!" It was strange how he'd use this term "Yankees," always kind of detaching himself from them. Well, he didn't come back to the States till after I left — but he kept writing me for quite a long time.

When I got to Porterville, Toni was carrying her fifth kid — the other four were all girls. So I helped out a lot with these little kids, taking them to the park and things like that. The youngest, Moni, was only a year-and-a-half; Beckie was three, Gracie four, and Darleen seven. They were really something — lively, always jackassing around and with a lot of character. I think spending time with them helped me a lot to come out of the real bad period I'd been through. We had a lot of fun picking grapes and plums together, and there were also some difficult times. Like when Gracie was helping me with the wash, putting the clothes through an old wringer. All of a sudden she started crying, "Mom! Mom!" I looked around and was she'd gotten her arm caught in the wringer. Toni came running, turned off the machine and we drove her to the hospital. Fortunately, it was just a minor sprain and they put her arm in a sling.

Then one day Toni was at the doctor's office getting her weekly check-up and I was looking after the kids. Gracie and Darleen were playing around trying to catch this bee and the two younger kids were watching. I was sitting with my mind way off somewhere and didn't even notice that the girls had gotten a couple of ice picks. Next thing I knew Gracie screamed and there was this terrible look on her face. She held her hand and I saw the ice pick sticking right through her finger. She pulled it out before I could get to her. It was bleeding pretty bad and I wrapped an old shirt around it. Then I phoned Arturo and asked if I should take her to the hospital. "Yes," he said, "and make sure they give her a tetanus shot!" So off I went with these four kids — Darleen holding on to Beckie while I held Moni on my shoulder and Gracie by her good hand. It was hotter than hell, about 108 in the shade and we were walking as fast as we could into town. We'd gone about a mile and the kids were really getting tired and cranky — especially Gracie, whose hand was bleeding again. Luckily, Toni came by in the car. She was really upset when she found out what had happened. Then we all piled into the car and drove Gracie to the hospital. They bandaged her hand and gave her a shot. I was pretty impressed with the kid because she never once cried or complained. The next morning Arturo asked if she wanted to go out back and catch some bees. "No! No! I don't want to catch no bees, daddy!" The next day he did the same thing, handing her an ice pick. She screamed out "No!" again, so I guess she'd learned her lesson with bees and ice picks.

I just couldn't help getting a fresher, healthier approach

to life being with those kids so much. Like when I'd been there only a few days and was sleeping on the couch, they all came and started jumping all over me. I turned over and told them to go away, but they still kept jumping and climbing on me, pulling my hair, pinching, tickling — harassing me constantly and pleading, "Come outside and play with us! Come on outside with us!" So finally I went outside, played with them a bit and laid down on the lawn. Then they turned the water hose on me. It was a favourite trick of theirs. I soon learned that Toni and Arturo let their kids run around wild, like animals. If you went into their room, they'd come jumping down all over you from their bunkbeds.

Anyway, I was getting involved with life again. I really had a gas with these kids. (I'd always liked other people's kids but still didn't think I wanted any of my own.) I talked with Toni a lot ... though never about Toronto. She was sort of straight and narrow, with a very small existence and very small thinking. She was almost ten years older than me — and more like a mother than a sister. It was different with me and Roger — who was a year older than me — and my two younger sisters. We were close in age and usually felt free to talk to one another. I think Toni knew something about my troubles in Toronto, but she never said anything. She probably thought it wasn't important enough to go into; that every kid goes through a period like that and I'd get over it and straighten out. The only thing she asked was whether I was going back to school. I said, "Oh, no — never!"

Sometimes Toni had these strange premonitions. One night before she went to bed she said, "Gee, I gotta feeling Peter's coming tomorrow." Peter was her half-brother who lived in B.C. "You're crazy," I said, "Peter's not going to come over a thousand miles to see you — probably doesn't have the bread for a trip like that. You haven't seen him for ten years and you probably won't see him for another ten!" She just said, "No, I think he's coming." Well, next morning I woke up to knocking at the door and sure enough it was ol' Pete. He comes in and I go running off to call Toni, yelling "He's here! He's here!" and thinking at the same time, "This is freakier than hell." Toni jumped out of bed and came rushing out as Pete and his wife Gertie came in. They stayed for five or six days and Art took his holidays. Every day we went swimming in this river. The water was really nice and cool compared to the hot summer air. I wasn't much of a swimmer but had lots of fun holding these heavy rocks and walking on the river bottom. The water level was dropping about three inches a day and after a few days the tops of our heads showed as we walked along the bottom.

Arturo was always kidding around and teasing, swatting me with a fly swatter and things like that. Well, the day before Pete and his wife left, we noticed Art sitting very still on the bank of the river as a dozen or so hornets buzzed around him. We were all laughing like crazy because he looked so strange sitting there and not moving a muscle. Then he let out this tremendous yell, "Aaahhh!" and slapped his forearm real hard. One of the hornets had bitten him. The kids were rolling around on the ground laughing and shouting, "Daddy's a sissy! Daddy's a sissy!" Arturo jumped up and dove into the river. The hornets had panicked him. We all laughed and teased him about it for at least a week.

Wally, this young guy I'd known a couple of summers before in Visalia, used to come over quite bit. He'd been in and out of jail since I last saw him. We'd usually go hiking and rattlesnake hunting. Up on this hill a few miles from the house was a snake pit. We'd go walking over there to see these baby rattlers, who weren't even old enough to have their rattles yet. Once, when we were looking at them, I heard this sound, like "swish-sh-ckicka-clicka, swish-sh, clicka," right behind me. I went peeling down the hill like mad. Wally was laughing and yelling, "Where are you going? It's only a cricket!" I stopped dead in my tracks feeling like a real idiot. "A cricket?" I thought. "Sure as hell sounded like a rattler to me!"

I kind of liked the small town, rural atmosphere of Porterville. It was more relaxing and easy-going than in big cities like Vancouver or Toronto. And in certain ways it appeared more productive too. Seemed like whatever you did in a small town left a mark, counted for something. Sometimes I'd work in the orange groves for these friends of Toni — Joan and Wayne. It was really fun and refreshing, checking on the sprinklers and doing other tasks. The groves were a real pleasure to work in; I loved the smell of oranges and even slept a few nights in the orchard. I could see that I was doing something productive ... useful. The oranges grew and ripened more each day and my work contributed to that process. I watched them grow and actually thought I could see the results of my labour in these ripening oranges. It was really different than working in some restaurant where there was no production — nothing growing — and you just did the same thing every day but got nowhere, like walking on a treadmill. When I was working at A&W, always running back and forth, it seemed that every day, every week, was the same; that I'd accomplished nothing. Run, run, run; but always in the same place.

In Porterville I also started reading a lot more. I read *Malcolm X Speaks* and was impressed with his intelligence, though I didn't necessarily agree with him. He was a practical man; he kept saying that a person had to *act*, to *do*. But

I wasn't interested then in doing, only in knowing. I thought I had to know something first, in case some day I wanted to do something. I read Malcolm's autobiography too. His ability to express himself really impressed me, but it also made me aware that my own vocabulary had dwindled. This bothered me, because when I was a kid I had a fantastic vocabulary and made A's in English until I was fifteen. That's when I started swearing a lot. After I quit school, it got worse; half my answers to questions were swear words. So I just lost my vocabulary; I didn't use it, so I lost it. Christ, it was pathetic. I tried to write a letter to my mom telling her I'd be coming home soon and ended up by writing, "Coming home." I couldn't think of anything else to say, or how to say it. Well, while I was reading I started building my vocabulary again, thinking it would be good if I could become articulate like Malcolm. At one time I had a bit of pride in my writing — not that I was great or anything — and I wanted to regain that pride. But it was very slow and difficult.

My sister Joan wrote me in Porterville, telling me about this NARP — the Native Alliance for Red Power — and sending me a copy of their newsletter ... which I thought was really sensational. She said the people in NARP, and especially this Ray Thom, were pretty smart and that I should meet and talk with them when I got back. This appealed to me. I'd never really voiced their sentiments, but I felt them. It was only in Toronto that I started using the term "honky" for whites. I used it a lot in Porterville, though, and my sister thought it was funny. It used to bother Arturo; he didn't like it at all. Toni'd just say I would be growing out of it soon. She had felt the same way as me once, but she'd mellowed and lost all her spunk.

I learned a lot by reading the newspaper too. There was

a lot of interesting stuff going on in the world at that time. The Vietnam war was getting hotter every day, and every week there'd be a report on how many Yanks had been killed. Toni was against the war and Art was for it. He'd say, "You're not an American; that's why you're against the war. Everybody's against the Americans!" Toni would answer, "Well, they should be! Your bloody army is tripping off everywhere, killing people, bombing little kids, even getting its own people killed. They stink!" But Art was a real patriot, getting up in the morning singing the National Anthem and things like that. It was a real contradiction: he wanted changes in the States, like a lot of liberal Americans, but he defended US imperialism. I used to think, "A real fascist; a typical American honky!" He was always saying that if we didn't like America we should fuck off to Russia or China. I asked him once, "What are you going to do if you wake up one day and find there are Commies all around, millions of Commies? Will you tell them all to go live in Russia? Soon you'll be here all by yourself!"

Well, that summer I did quite a bit of thinking. I realized how sickening Arturo was and it started getting very uncomfortable. Toni was different; she was easy going, not too intellectual, hard working and a person of high standards who didn't expect others to be the same. We would often disagree on things and sometimes argue, but she always let bygones be bygones and we got along pretty well. But it got bad with Arturo. I couldn't stand his sick jokes or his patriotism any more and decided to leave very soon. Then I got this letter from my mom, saying she was very ill and asking me to come home and help her around the house. I gave Toni about $100 that I had saved in a Vancouver bank and took the next bus home. All in all, it had been a good summer for me. I was off dope, dried out, thinking and reading more and about to enter a new kind of life.

Red Power

I came back from Porterville at the end of August 1968 — I think it was the 27th — and stayed at my parents' place in North Vancouver. The family situation had changed quite a bit. My brothers weren't living there anymore (Ed was still in Toronto and Rog was working up at Powell River), my dad was off fishing with Gordie like he'd done the summer before, Joan and Joyce hardly spoke to each other — they were in separate bedrooms and I slept downstairs — and my mom was unusually quiet. The place seemed almost like a morgue, which was strange since the family was usually pretty vivacious or gregarious. I asked my mom what the problem was. "I've got cancer," she said. "They're going to operate next month but they can't promise it will cure me. The kids don't know yet — and don't tell them."

This really shocked me. She'd had this malignant tumour for well over a year and the doctors feared the cancer might have spread too far to be cured. She might die. And this really scared me. I'd have to raise my two younger brothers and Al, this fourteen-year-old kid whom mom adopted when he was ten. I'd have to take care of the three of them till they were eighteen, and this thought really changed me — made me think more seriously about getting a job and becoming more stable.

Mom talked about the girls quite a bit. She said that they'd gone out one night in July and Joan came back bruised and with a cut on her head. "I asked them what happened but they wouldn't tell me the truth. Why don't you try to talk with them, Bobbi?" Later that first week I did;

I talked to both of them in Joyce's room, sitting on her bed. I asked what had happened with this Mike — Joyce's boyfriend at the time — and the guy who took Joan out. Joan started crying right away and Joyce practically became hysterical. When they'd calmed down a bit Joan told me the story — or as much of it as she remembered. "Mike came over with this guy Steve and they asked us if we wanted to go for a ride. We drove out to Horseshoe Bay and parked. Steve asked me if I wanted to take a walk down to the railroad tracks and I said okay. Joyce and Mike stayed behind sitting on a log, talking. When we were about half a mile down the path, Steve grabbed me and threw me down on the ground. He started kissing and mauling me and I struggled to get away from him. Then he started slapping me around, hitting me and tearing at my clothes. I screamed for help but he put his hand over my mouth and clubbed me with this big rock. Joyce can tell you the rest."

"Well," said Joyce, "When Mike and I heard a scream we thought maybe Joan had fallen or something and gotten hurt. We ran down the hill and found her lying on the ground unconscious with this guy Steve raping her. I yelled at Mike to do something but he just stood there like he was frozen. Steve got up and said, 'Let's drive them over to my place!' Mike said he wanted to take us home but Steve became very angry and threatened him. So they drove us over to Steve's place and I helped Joan get cleaned up. Steve told Joan that if she said anything about what'd happened he'd kill her. We both believed he might do it, so when mom asked questions later we didn't tell her anything."

I was really angry. "That guy should be hung!" I said "Why the hell didn't you tell mom? She'd have called the cops and that bastard might have gotten what he deserves."

Joan started crying again. She was only sixteen and she

was really ashamed about the whole thing — even about going out with the guy, whom she'd never met before. She'd also picked up on this whole Christian ethic from my mom and that made her feel more and more guilty and ashamed as the weeks passed. Joan was always pretty shy and withdrawn, but this thing with Steve made her worse than ever. She and Joyce hardly spoke to each other; I think just looking at one another reminded them of Horseshoe Bay. They'd never been very close, but now they were really alienated. Joyce was spending a lot of time with a guy named Brian McLellan who'd been taking her out for three years and wanted to marry her. Joan became real introverted. She didn't even go out with a guy for several months after being raped.

My brother Gordie came home alone in early September. The old man had left him stranded on the docks up north for two weeks with no food and only a little money. Gordie was only fourteen and being left like that really upset him. Finally he was able to borrow enough money from a friend of my dad's to fly home — which was the only other way of getting home except by boat. The old man came home a week or so later and things really got tense. Joyce and Joan were estranged; Gordie was upset and angry; mom's operation was postponed till November; and the old man was living down in the basement and always ranting and raving — especially at me.

I started looking for work soon after I got home and finally found a job at this Tomahawk drive-in, on the north shore of Capilano Reserve. The owner was a really weird character, a liberal who was heavy on the traditions and history of the area. He had all these old muskets, gold panning gear and Indian artifacts which he'd collected over thirty years. He even named his hamburgers and other things after different chiefs from the north shore. Most of the staff were Indians. I worked five hours a day, five days a week — mainly as a grill cook and dishwasher in the kitchen, but sometimes as a waitress. The work wasn't too hard. It was a kind of a fancy restaurant and not that busy most of the time. People had to pay quite a bit for their "Indian hamburgers."

The old man was getting pretty bad, wanted me to leave as soon as I got a job. Ed was back from Toronto and the place seemed to be in a continual turmoil. I couldn't hack being around the old man any more but I couldn't leave because of mom. When he yelled at me to get out, I'd just yell back, "Why don't you get out? You've got a place of your own in Coquitlam. Why don't you go live there? You know you're not welcome here!" He'd have loved to boot me out but didn't dare try. Even when I was young I never took any shit from him. My grandfather always told me : "Never take what you think you don't deserve." So no matter what shit I got, I always held on to my position "being bad" just to get back at the old man. He was really sadistic ... sick in the head. Like a few times when I was washing the floor he'd intentionally step on my hands. I learned over the years that the more insolent I was with him, the less courage he'd have to do anything about it.

I'd known the old man was a racist before, mainly by the way he treated mom, but it really came home to me when I started dating this guy named Johnny, who was half Indian half Black. I brought him to the house one day and the old man didn't even say hello; he just grunted and went down to the basement. Later he and mom had a real argument. She battled it out with him and he grabbed her and was about to push her down the stairs when I stepped in and slapped him real hard on the face. Then the shit started flying. We argued back and forth, screaming at each other and him making all these racist remarks about dirty squaws, niggers and so on. It really hit me all at once that the old man had all these racist sentiments. I think it was aggravated by the fact that only two of the boys were "white" while the rest of us were definitely "Indian." My mom was only half Indian, but she had affairs with other men on the Reserve when dad was off somewhere — which was quite often. So he resented having to support all of mom's "illegitimate" children — though in fact he did bloody little to support us. Anyway, for some strange reason he didn't want any of us kids to marry Indians or Blacks. And when he met Johnny he just flipped out, screaming that he didn't want me going out with guys like that. "They're just going to get you pregnant!" he said "It takes two to get pregnant," I replied. "It doesn't happen by magic!"

My sister Joyce was really a bitch at this time. She was planning to marry this Brian — who was white — and the old man had promised her some land for their wedding present. So, even though my mom had cancer, Joyce always took the old man's side. I told her, "you know he's sick in the head and has done bloody nothing for us all these years except give out abuse!" But she was real selfish, only interested in the land he'd promised her. The rest of us didn't mean anything to her.

It wasn't long after I'd been home that Joan told me about this meeting she'd been to with my brother Ed. I was called by this Howard Adams, a half-breed from Saskatchewan who was a professor at Saskatoon University. He'd started a militant mass organization called the Saskatchewan Native Action Committee which was involved in school boycotts, demonstrations and so on. Joan said he was a Red Power advocate and sounded pretty interesting. She also told me about a local group called the Native Alliance for Red Power (NARP) and who the people were: Henry Mack, Gerri and Gordie Andrew, Wayne and Ray Thom and their sister Sue. This little group put out a newsletter and when I read their first issue it sounded pretty good to me. The main theme seemed to be: "We don't need Whites!" — sort of an anti-white culture thing along with a demand for Red Power. They also wrote about their first demonstration, which was against religious, mainly Catholic, schools. They called it "cultural genocide" and objected to schools not allowing Indians to speak and be taught in their own languages.

I told Joan I'd like to attend one of their meetings. "Sure," she said, "they hold them on Tuesday nights." Then she made a phone call and arranged for someone to pick me up. The following Tuesday Gordie came by for me with Ray and we drove down to Hastings Street. He said they were meeting above China Arts & Crafts in the Progressive Workers' Movement (PWM) offices, where NARP had its newsletter printed. As we went in we passed through the back of this pub. I remember Ray asking me if I wanted to go for a wet. I never heard that expression before and thought maybe he wanted to go to the bathroom. So I said, "Sure, I'll wait for you here." Then he explained and said, "Maybe we should go get the others." We went out front, but I still wasn't quite sure what his intentions were. Gordie and Gerri were there but Gerri said she wasn't old enough to get in. She was only twenty and couldn't pass for older; her baby face made her look fifteen. Ray said, "Well, why don't we just pick up a case and bring it upstairs?" By that time others had arrived and everyone agreed.

The PWM offices were on the second floor. They had a printing press and, off on a landing, a section for collating and stapling. A few PWM guys were there, along with about six NARP members. They were talking about Cuba and the Vietnamese revolution and as I looked around the place my eyes fell on a barrel of rifles standing in the corner. Wayne Thom was sitting there on top of them and I thought, "Christ! All this talk about revolution and here are all these rifles!" I was a bit scared but didn't know quite what to think of it. (About a week later I asked Ray about the guns and he said they belonged to the PWM and not NARP.)

That first night I helped collate and staple their newsletter. People were talking and arguing all the time: about politics; about some guy who was coming over from Vancouver Island to speak, and a soccer game that was planned between the PWM and NARP on the weekend. There was a lot of teasing and joking going on, along with the work and beer drinking. It really wasn't much of a meeting; mainly a work session. When we'd finished they told me they were planning to sell the newsletter around town, especially at the Indian Centre dances. They also mentioned that they had this discussion group at the Centre in which NARP people participated. It was on Friday and they asked me to come along.

I went to the Andrew's place for the next meeting. We went downstairs and they were playing this tape by Stokely Carmichael. I noticed that everybody was drinking; in fact, Wayne Thom had already passed out. I thought it was pretty strange, but I didn't say anything. People drank and I didn't have anything against drinking.

The tape was about an hour and a half long and I listened to it carefully. Everyone laughed when Stokely was talking about Black people dyeing their hair, trying to straighten it, and girls putting on magnolia cream to look more white. It set me to thinking. I could remember when I was in school, how I always set my hair and wanted it to look curly — but it never lasted very long, the curls falling out in an hour or so. It always made me feel bad. And when I was sixteen I used to pluck my eyebrows to look more attractive by white standards. So I related to what Stokely had to say pretty well.

After the tape was over there was a discussion. Gordie did most of the talking; seemed he remembered everything on the tape and I thought he must have heard it several times before. He'd use some quote from Chairman Mao and relate it to a point Stokely made. At that time I knew nothing whatsoever about Mao Tse-tung and just sat there wondering what he was talking about. He kept talking about the "little red book" and repeating that "political power grows out of the barrel of a gun." That seemed to be his favourite saying. Gordie was a white guy, but because he was married to Gerri — who was an Indian like all the others — they allowed him to be a member of NARP. He was also very close to PWM, though I wasn't sure at that time whether he was a member or just a supporter.

Ray Thom started arguing with him about how PWM people went around quoting Chairman Mao and doing very little else. "It's not good to keep on quoting and quoting! You can't learn Marxism by a mechanical process where you just go on quoting things till they stick." They talked and argued back and forth for about two hours and nobody else got to say anything, just sat and listened.

When it was over, people just went home. I stayed behind for a while talking to Gerri. She seemed a pretty sensible person and knowledgeable about different struggles going on. She talked about Vietnam and about how the Iroquois Confederacy had gone to the World Court to protest their people being drafted and sent to Vietnam against their will. They'd finally won their case. She also told me about some other people who were Red Power advocates: Larry Seymore, Duke Redbird — who was in some Saul Alinsky films — and Harold Cardinal. By the way she talked I felt that a lot was going on and that I was really out of it — behind the times. Finally, I said I had to go home and left. Stacy, who'd come to the discussion with me, drove me back to my mom's place.

I went to several NARP meetings after that. Most of the time I either talked to Gerri or listened to Ray and Gordie arguing. It almost seemed there was a personal thing between them. Once Gerri asked me if I wanted to go sell newspapers with her. NARP got the Panther paper and sold them up at Simon Fraser University (SFU) and the University of British Columbia (UBC). So I went up to SFU with her and was selling *The Black Panther* when a guy named Jamie Reed came up and started attacking us as being counter-revolutionaries and so forth. He was a member of the Internationalists, which later changed their name to the Communist Party of Canada, Marxist-Leninist (CPC-ML). I remember being taken aback because I didn't even know what a counter-revolutionary was — or that I was supposed to be a revolutionary in the first place. Finally I got mad. He was leaning against our table and screaming things in my face. "Just get out of here," I told him in a serious voice, "before I flatten you!" Gerri had been trying to reason with him but it was my experience with screamers that at some point or other they ended up taking a swing at you. Gerri was talking calmly about Black Power, what it was, and that NARP supported it. Then just as she was telling him he had no right to call her counter-revolutionary, some student came up and made some stupid comment about how proletarian poetry wasn't poetry at all. This diverted Jamie and, in the meantime, people started coming up and buying newspapers, curious to see what was going on. We sold out in a couple of hours and went home. On the way I asked Gerri who this guy Jamie was and she said, "Oh, they're all a bunch of crazies, these Internationalists. They go around quoting Mao and acting like a bunch of gangsters, beating up on people, just trying to intimidate everyone into agreeing with their line."

The next day we took some more papers out to the University of British Columbia and raised quite a stir. UBC was really a conservative school — still is — and there were a lot of anti-Panther people who came up and argued with us. One guy, a real racist, tried to intimidate us by saying things like, "Hell, what do you Indians know, anyway?" We just laughed at him, angry but thinking he was pretty stupid. This was my first experience with that type of political action — trying to engage in political discussion and so on. Actually, I didn't do much of the talking, but I listened a lot to Gerri and helped out where I could. She seemed to know what she was talking about and I respected her for it. On the way back I asked her how she came to know so much about the Panthers, Vietnam and so forth. She said she'd read quite a few books and things and gave me a reading list. I expressed some interest, but didn't really pick up on it right away.

Fish-In!

For the first few weeks I just assumed that Sue Thom was Ray's wife and I was pretty surprised when he phoned and asked me out one night. "Where's Sue?" I asked. "Oh, she's out at Agassiz with the folks." I told him I'd consider it. "Shit," I thought, "I don't want to get caught up in a situation like this, even if they're separated!" Later, I went over to see Gerri and after we'd been talking for a while I asked, "Who's this Sue Thom, anyway?" "Sue?" she replied. "Oh, she's Ray's little sister; been out of town for a time visiting her folks on the Reserve."

When Ray asked me out again I said okay. At first I wasn't sure how I felt about him. He seemed intelligent, nice to be with, and I found him sort of attractive. But he was quiet and moody and seemed real uneasy around whites — especially Gordie Andrew. It was strange, because intellectually he wasn't anti-white, he was just uneasy around them. Worse, though, was his drinking; it seemed to me that he was never drunk but always drinking.

Our first date was on a Saturday night and he asked me if I wanted to go to a nightclub. He was all dressed up and kind of surprised when I said, "Hell no! I hate those joints." There were two other couples with us: Stacy and Dave Hanuse; and my sister Joan and Jerry Jones, whom I thought was kind of haywire. For some reason Joan was attracted to him. I thought maybe she was a bit masochistic after her ordeal, but it really bugged me the way she let this Jerry abuse her.

The six of us drove out to Stanley Park with this apricot

brandy. Everybody but me was getting looped as they kept passing the bottle around. We parked near the beach and got out. I liked the challenge of running on the beach, sinking into the sand and splashing through the water. "Let's have a race!" I said. We all started running, but some weren't too enthusiastic. I practically had to pull Ray along and Dave did the same with Stacy. Then, as we were running through this slime — seaweed and muck on the rocks — Ray tripped and went sliding along on his bum. It was really funny. Here he was, wearing these black slacks and white shirt, looking just like a bureaucrat who'd fallen of his horse into the mud. (From then on I always bugged Ray about the way he dressed, saying things like: "You look like a bloody faggot in those clothes! Why don't you wear jeans like a man!" I guess I was pretty obnoxious; don't know why he bothered with me at all.) Anyway, Ray was laughing right along with the rest of us. And we laughed all the way home. It had been a lot of fun, and wasn't the last time we went out to Stanley Park.

When we got back to Ray's place this Gordie started giving him a rough time. At first, Ray was ashamed of having Gordie see him all coated with slime and wanted to sneak in the back way. We talked him out of it, however, saying, "Ah, don't worry about it — just slap him down if he says anything." Well, Gordie was pretty much a loud-mouth and started bugging Ray right away. "Boy," he said, "you must have gone to some nightclub." He kept on ribbing Ray, who just smiled and led us to his room. Gordie and Gerri lived upstairs and Ray and another guy rented rooms in the basement.

A while later I talked to my mom about Ray; about the good times we were having and how nice a guy he was. She listened, then said: "He must be something pretty special. I never heard you talk about any other guy like this. You'll probably end up marrying him." For some reason, this made me angry. "That's the farthest thing from my mind!" I said. "You think I want to raise eight or ten kids like you did — end up a baby manufacturer?" "And where might you be if I didn't have a bunch of kids?" she asked, kind of insulted. Not wanting to upset her, I backed off a bit. "Well, I just don't want to spend my whole life raising kids."

I started going around with Ray after our first date. I liked him quite a bit but we had plenty of arguments and his drinking bothered me. He had started back to school at Vancouver City College in September and every morning he'd drink a bottle of wine, go to school, come back, drink some more wine, then go to bed. It was really getting bad after a while and I didn't like it at all. I was just getting over a rough time with dope and didn't want to get sucked into drinking as a substitute — which I knew would be easy enough to do. So whenever he offered me some wine, I'd say, "Oh no! Not for me!"

At one of the Indian Centre discussions I met this Larry Seymore. He was kind of an orator; he could get up at the drop of a hat and make a long and usually interesting speech. He gave us a talk on fishing rights and about the people in his area who were getting arrested just for fishing like they always did. At that point someone mentioned that the Nisqually people were planning a fish-in at the end of October and welcomed all the help they could get. Soon everybody seemed to be talking about different things — treaty rights, fish-ins, arrests, Indians getting beaten up, and so forth. The discussion just floated along with seemingly no direction. I just listened. Then a guy named Harry, who was supposed to be the discussion leader, got up and made a big speech about how he'd been a real drunk before, then joined

139

the AA — it was like a pitch for any alcoholics there to join up. After a while every body told him to shut up and sit down. The meeting was really getting out of hand — everyone wanted to talk and take action on the particular things that bothered them.

In the meantime, the Indian Centre board of directors was becoming really paranoid about Red Power people coming to the Centre all the time. Finally, one of them got up and said NARP wouldn't be allowed to hold any more discussions there since Ray had asked people to go down to Nisqually. It didn't matter much, because all we did was go there and have informal discussions. After awhile, however, they barred Ray from the Centre altogether and NARP wasn't allowed to sell its newsletter there, attend dances, and so on. I was pretty confused, trying to figure out what was going on, why people were being barred for talking about things that didn't seem to me to be very harmful.

I worked at the Tomahawk for about two months. Stacy worked not too far away at an A&W. She had this really nice '66 Chev — which she always went bombing around town in — and often after work she'd come over to the Tomahawk to see me. She was quite a character and very funny when she got going ... telling jokes, doing imitations, simulating situations and so on. Once a bunch of us were down on Stanley Park beach and she was drawing these pictures in the sand. "Here's a cop," she said, and drew a picture of a Mountie with his eyes crossed and hat on crooked. He really looked funny. Then she drew an Indian and put a stick down between them, saying: "And here's an Indian. The cop takes this stick and goes clunk, clunk, clunk, — right on the Indian's head." Then she started acting out all these situations she'd been in. Like when we went into this pub and she said, "Two beers, please." The waiter looked at her and said,"We don't serve Indians in here." Stacy then looked at him real seriously and said, "But I didn't order an Indian, I asked for two beers." Then we both burst out laughing and the waiter started screaming "Get out of here!" livid with rage. Stacy just bounded out of the pub with her usual big smile and off we went.

Stacy also knew a lot of Black jive; the way Blacks — at least in Toronto — talk to each other. I never did catch on to it. They seemed to be speaking English, but I could never understand what they were saying. So I usually just sat in silence, not knowing what the hell was going on. But Stacy was good at it, really good. She could carry on and on with it while we laughed and tried to understand. It was very funny.

Not long before my mom was due to go into the hospital, Jerry Jones called up and asked Joan if she could come to a party. It was after midnight and a dance at the Indian Centre had just ended. Mom wouldn't let her go unless I agreed to go with her, and Joan said she wouldn't go without me, that she was still scared. "Well fuck," I said, "you're going to have to go out by yourself sometime, you know." But she just kept saying, "You've got to come with me Bobbi." "Oh, shit!" I thought. "All I need is a party." I was reading a book Ray bought me by Fanon, *Black Skin, White Mask.* "You're crazy," I said. "Almost one o'clock and you want to go to a party!" She kept pleading and finally I gave in to my mom's urgings: "It would be nice if you took her to the party, Bobbi, she hasn't been out for some time now." "OK, fuck it! But I don't see what it's got to do with me." "Don't keep saying that awful word, Bobbi!" my mom said. She had been getting angry at my swearing, which seemed to be getting worse now that Ray was trying to get me to quit.

Joan lit up when I said I'd go. "Oh, good! I'll go change," and she ran into the bedroom. You have to understand that Joan was always changing clothes; whenever she went out of the house, even to the store, she changed. I yelled after her: "Joan, you're fine! Let's just go!" "Oh no," she replied, "I've got to change" — from one thing to another. She was kind of neurotic about her clothes and had a closet as long as her room full of them. I went up and found her trying on all these things — like a bloody fashion model. I just stood and watched, wearing my pair of green jeans and a green sweater, which was about all I owned. Finally, she was ready; dressed up slick and shiny and standing in front of the mirror making up her eyes and putting on lipstick, make-up and so on. I thought, "Christ, she's put on just like a little doll! It's embarrassing." She was still touching up her face and I said, "OK, you're fine. Just like a toy. Now let's go."

The two guys and some other friends were waiting outside in a car. I guess they'd been drinking pretty heavy all night, cause when I opened the door to get in, Ray fell right out onto the side walk. "Christ," I said, "what a stupid-ass party this is going to be!" All the way there in the car I was bitching about starting a party so late. Everyone just listened, feeling uncomfortable ... except for Jerry, who was always fine no matter what. He and Joan were carrying on in the back seat and he asked: "What's wrong, babe? what happened?" When we got to Gordie's place it was full of people and beer. Gordie was drunk as hell; he drank as much as Ray and I thought that was the only reason they got along at all. Ray straightened up a bit after we got there and the two of us just talked off in a corner. He started telling me the story of his life. Soon everybody fell asleep so Gordie drove us home. It was a short lived party.

During this period I went to several NARP meetings and became a regular member. It was ridiculous at first because everybody got drunk. I complained about the drinking after a while and we had a big discussion. Finally, everyone agreed that there would be no more drinking at meetings. NARP had started at the end of 1967 with a really racist/traditionalist position, printing 5,000 copies of a dinky newsletter full of this kind of thinking. The newsletter, Native Alliance for Red Power, came out irregularly and the intervals were long enough so that you could see some political changes had taken place between any two issues. We were influenced pretty much by the Panther line and also had some contact with leftist groups. Aside from the PWM people, who printed our newsletter and were Maoists, we had some dealings with the Trotskyists. One guy, Dave Cuthand, used to talk to me quite a bit. He was a Cree from Saskatchewan where they named you after some major event. His great grandfather had been cut in the hand during the Riel Rebellion. So they nicknamed him Cuthand and the name was passed on to his children and grandchildren. Anyway, Doug's father was a reverend and Doug was a member of the Young Socialist Alliance (YSA), a Trotskyist organization. Sue Thom was also a member and Ray had been on the margins for a while, then quit. So, toward the end of 1968, NARP was slowly becoming a more serious organization, beginning to move beyond social drinking and idle conversation to do some organizing work in the Indian Community and trying to start a few programs like the discussion at the Indian Centre.

About a week before we were to leave for the Nisqually fish-in, Joan, Ray, Stacy, Jim Dixon (a white friend of ours) and I went over to my place with a case of beer. My mom had already gone into the hospital and when my dad saw us come in the door he charged toward me and screamed: "Get these people out of here! And take that beer with you!" "What's the trouble?" I asked, keeping as calm as possible. "You take those Indians and beer out of here! And you, Joan, you stay home! It's too late for you to be going out!" I thought, "What? She's sixteen years old and it's only 8:30!" "OK," I said, "but I want to take my other half case of beer with me." As I went to get the beer I whispered to Joan that she should sneak out the bathroom window and we'd pick her up down the street in about fifteen minutes. On my way out I noticed my other sister Joyce sitting in the front room with her boyfriend and a half emptied bottle of Scotch. "Hmm," I thought, "so it's alright for them to drink, eh?"

We drove away, then came back a few minutes later and started looking for Joan. The old man was out too, going up and down the street calling her. We figured she was hiding in the bushes out back, afraid to show herself, and after waiting down the street for about half-an-hour we decided she'd given up. When we got over to Ray's we phoned Rog and asked him to call the house and see if Joan was there. He was living in North Van with his wife Donna. He called back an hour or so later and said that Joan had walked the four and a half miles over to his place and had just arrived. We went over and picked her up, but decided it was best if she spent the night with Rog and Donna.

Next day we visited my mom in the hospital and asked if Joan and I could go down to the Nisqually fish-in near Seattle with Ed and my younger brother Gord. She said "OK," and we left for the fish-in in a few days, not going home again and spending our nights at Rog's and Ray's.

On October 27th a bunch of us left for Nisqually, which

was near Olympia in Washington. There were Ed, Gord, Joan and me, Ray and Sue Thom and Henry Mack. The first thing we did was go to this Chuck Sweet's house in Seattle to find out exactly how to get to the fish-in. Chuck was an older white guy who worked as a longshoreman and seemed to have a lot of interest in Native rights and the left in general. There was a guy from the Congress of Racial Equality (CORE) there and we got into a big discussion with him. Ray was talking about the proletarian revolution, about how the working class was revolutionary and so on, and this Ron had kind of a Black Muslim line. He was saying mainly that white people were devils heading for destruction and there was no way of saving them. It seemed like more of a religious than a political way of thinking. Ray hadn't really gone into Marx on his own at this time; he mainly picked up on what Gordie Andrew and other leftists in the PWM and YSA were saying. Pretty soon it got to be an argument between Ron and Ray and me, because after listening for an hour or so I found I didn't agree with either of them and was getting worked up. I didn't believe in devils, so it didn't make any sense to me to call white people devils. What did it really mean? At the same time, I didn't agree with Ray that the Canadian working class was going to lead the struggle — especially the Indian struggle. And it really got to me emotionally when he said North American workers weren't racist, or that working class solidarity against capitalism somehow prevented white workers from being affected by racism. This ran counter to all my experience and I got pretty wrought up.

"I've lived in working class neighbourhoods most of my life," I said, "and it was working class kids who beat up on me all through school. They hated Indians; in fact they were the most racist of all. Middle class white liberal racism is mainly paternalistic, but with workers and their kids, they either ignored us or abused us."

"These divisions," Ray would calmly reply, "have been brought about by capitalism." But he couldn't explain how; it all seemed to be some kind of accident. My experience just wouldn't let me accept these wooden arguments about proletarian unity and revolution.

"Look, do you want me to believe that those guys I had so much trouble with, who went over to the Reserve looking for Indian women — raping and plundering — are going to make a revolution to free us all from oppression? You gotta be kidding! It wasn't very long ago when we'd pick up our phone and hear these workers talking about the 'half breed Lee pigs' — meaning Joan, Joyce, Toni and me. Not once did a white ask me out on a regular date; it was always, 'hey, you want to go for a ride up the mountain?' We all knew what that meant, so I never had a single date with a white neighbourhood kid all through junior high school."

(Once my brother Rog picked up the phone and heard a couple of his white school "friends" refer to us as the "Lee half-breeds" and "little Lee squaws." They said we were pretty snotty for Indians because we wouldn't let them lay us and stuff like that. Well, this really shocked Rog. He never had any white school friends after that. He became real cynical and refused to say a word at school during his whole last year. Finally, they kicked him out because he nearly drove one of his teachers insane with his silence. He even became quiet at home and even now he doesn't talk much with people. After leaving school he got a job with some Punjabis and just worked and kept to himself. We were surprised when he and Donna got together.)

Ray was really strange at this time. Like he'd talk about proletarian revolution and all that but write things for the

NARP newsletter which were real cultural-nationalist. It didn't seem to him that there was any contradiction; and it was the same with Gordie Andrew. After a while I thought they were almost making fun of the newsletter, especially Gordie. They'd say one thing, or take one line, on the "outside," then engage in this almost bizarre political exhibitionism in their writing. Gordie had been in the PWM but was expelled because of his line on culture. He still maintained friendly relations with them and shared most of their views on the working class and so forth. Anyway, I was kind of confused and upset when listening to Ray's arguments and then remembering what he had written in the last newsletter.

Chuck Sweet acted like a moderator for this discussion at his place and finally, at around 2 a.m., we went to bed without settling anything — which was usually the case. In the morning we drove down to Frank's Landing on the Nisqually River about forty miles from Olympia. We entered along a road paralleling the river which divided the Reserve into two parts. First we came to Bill Frank's house. There was a trailer surrounded by cleared land on which a lot of tents had been set up. One was a big powwow tent which could hold at least sixty people. Nearer the narrow bridge which connected the two halves of the Reserve was the Bridges's house. We crossed the bridge and set up our tent near some others in a kind of hollow. Two nets had been set up, one near Frank's trailer and the other close to the Bridges's house.

We met some of the people who lived there — Al and Maiselle Bridges and their daughters, Suzette and Val — then started helping out by gutting and cleaning fish. The Bridges were one of very few families that lived permanently on the Reserve. The McClouds, who were related to the

Bridges, also lived there. In addition, there were a lot of people from a neighbouring Reserve, who were also Puyallups, as well as some hippies and members of the Seattle Liberation Front. I talked mainly with a couple of girls named Marcy and Roxanne; they were Indians but had some sort of relations with the Panthers. Later that day two of these guys, Curtis Harris and another named Dixon, came down to the fish-in all dressed up in their Panther uniforms. They just went around talking to people. Then Buffy Sainte-Marie came and talked about how violence was bad and that kind of stuff. She was a pretty well-known folk singer. Finally, Jane Fonda arrived with her own press corps. There was a buzz of reporters all over her, snapping pictures whenever she'd do anything. She'd pick up a fish and smile — "click, click, click"; go help pull in a net — "click, click, click." It was really ridiculous and left a bad impression on me. Buffy was pretty much the same way.

It was cloudy and raining most of the time we were there. After the fishing and other work, people sat around talking. We were all pretty tired, not having slept much the night before, and decided to go get some sleep. So we went to our tent and crawled into our sleeping bags. At about 2 in the morning I woke up to the blast of horns, which was the signal in the event of trouble. A bunch of white vigilantes had been coming up from Seattle to harass people at the fish-in, so guards were posted and warning system set up. Our tent had been leaking and everything was damp. It was dark out, cold and rainy. We heard a lot of ruckus and crossed the bridge to see what was going on. By the time we got there a mass brawl was under way. Everyone was fighting. I saw Val hitting some white guy with a paddle — knocked him right out. My little brother Gord was all excited, giving me a blow-by-blow account and telling me who the best fighters were. Then this Black guy from CORE, Ron, got up and started shouting for people to stop fighting. There was a calm, then the fighting broke out again. The vigilantes only left when they heard that help was coming in from the outside. They saw these flares go up and split in their cars.

Suzette was telling me that these white high school kids had been using a deserted part of the Reserve for drinking and fooling around. They'd drive up with their cases of beer and have a party. Since the fish-in, however, the Puyallup didn't allow any more drinking on the Reserve. She thought this was the main reason for the harassment.

It was raining so bad, and our tent was so wet, that we decided we might as well stay up and talk. A lot of people went into the powwow tent and were talking around a big fire. I talked to a number of people and learned quite a bit. Most of the Puyallup called themselves traditionalists. They were kind of religious, belonging to this Peyote Church. I'd never heard of it before, but noticed they would have these ceremonies and smoke peyote apart from the others. Al Bridges was an old guy with really long hair. I asked him why he let his hair get so long and he said, "We always had long hair before the whites made us cut it. I've not cut mine since 1956. It's the Indian way." Maiselle Bridges and the girls had a really humble approach to people, which impressed me quite a bit. When they were attacked they would fight back like demons, but otherwise they were very calm and had a real good comportment. I found their humble, all-suffering character really strange.

Next morning Gord noticed this Seattle hippie wrecking one of the nets, dragging it over the bottom and putting holes in it. He jumped up and started telling the guy he should leave the net alone, that he was just damaging it. The guy pretended he didn't hear a word, just kept dragging the net along. "Hey, stop buggering up the net!" Gord shouted. "Just leave it alone!" "Shove off, kid. I know what I'm doing." But Gord kept yelling and the guy was getting angry. He dropped the net and gave Gord a push. I was getting angry too and walked up saying, "Get your hands off that net you big ass! Can't you see you're putting holes in it?" He just stood there with a surprised look on his face as Gord skillfully set the net and pulled it in again. He'd been fishing all his life and was used to much larger nets than that one.

That afternoon there was a demonstration at the Capitol in Olympia. I slept all the way there. The rain had stopped. Most of the militants there were women and three of them did most of the speaking — Roxanne, Suzette and Marcy Hall. They were traditionalists so there was nothing unusual about women acting as spokesmen for the group. In fact, they told me they were having trouble getting the men involved. The only man who spoke was Hank Adams, who'd been to university and wasn't traditional.

Marcy was sort of a self-styled revolutionary. She had a Panther approach, saying things like "All power to the people!" "We got to get it on!" and so forth. Roxanne talked a lot about Indian rights to determine how they fished, how much they would sell. She told about the Bridges, how they'd been beaten up several times by State troopers. Suzette went into more detail about their treaty rights. Then they took this fish and some demands up to Governor Evans. I don't know if he received them personally or not.

Seems the main issue was that the fishing and other rights guaranteed by the Medicine Creek Treaty were being violated by the government. The treaty said that the Indians had the right to fish "as long as the grass grows" — forever and ever. The State, however, kept imposing regulations on their fishing, arguing things about conservation and so forth. The Puyallup wanted to practice their own methods of conservation and complained about sport fishermen being allowed to fish all year round while they were being prohibited from doing commercial net fishing. They had a good case because a Federal Supreme Court ruling had reaffirmed that all their treaty rights should be recognised. But the State of Washington didn't agree; they would arrest people for commercial fishing, put them through county and State courts and then drop the charges as soon as the case was appealed to the Federal court. They kept passing this illegal legislation restricting Indian fishing rights, then harassing people with game wardens, state troopers, court actions, and so on.

It was a real waste of money and time — both of which the government has a lot of and the Indians didn't.

I reacted to the obvious injustice of the thing and was furious. I was also impressed by how militant and courageous most of the Puyallup were, their willingness to stand up against the forces of "law and order." I wasn't too hot on the traditionalism, however, especially the Shaker religion and peyote smoking. They didn't push it, though; didn't even talk about their religion or ceremonies unless they thought you were interested in becoming a member. I wasn't. Still being a bit paranoid about dope, I didn't want to get caught up in any peyote cult. After every minor victory or set back they held a peyote ceremony and there was lots of singing, dancing and bell ringing.

When we returned to the fish-in camp we learned that ninety fish and game wardens had been there and confiscated all our belongings — fishing nets and gear, every little thing. They'd also arrested three men: Al Bridges, a Navaho

Street Patrol

Once the bail had been paid, we started back for Vancouver, getting home around 7 p.m. We went straight to my place and the old man was still there. As soon as he saw Joan and me he became furious; must have been brooding and, perhaps, worrying the whole seven or eight days we were gone, heating up to the explosion point. He started off on Joan, yelling at her and was just about to hit her when I pushed her out of the way and said, "Look, if you're going to smash Joan around, you'll have to smash me too! It was me who asked her to come along." Then he started hollering at Ed and me. We told him to calm down, that we'd told mom we were going to the fish-in and she said it was okay. But he kept getting madder. Said if I looked by my door I'd find my suitcase. "Go fill it and get out!" he shouted.

So I took the suitcase into my room and started packing. I could hear Joyce arguing with Joan; telling her she shouldn't hang around with me, that I was a bad influence on her, that she should smarten up, and so forth. Then Joyce came into my room and started yelling and asking why I'd taken Joan down to the States. "Mom said it was alright," I said, "and it's none of your business anyway. You're not her mother, you know!" But she kept acting very self righteous about the whole situation. She was a "nice girl" and Joan and I weren't; we should behave ourselves and listen to our father like she did.

Joan and Gord came in and both were crying; they wanted to go away with me, move away from the old man. Soon we were all mad at Joyce and screaming at her. She went out and slammed the door. I was finished packing and went downstairs. Ed was telling Joyce to mind her own business; Joan and Gord were still saying they wanted to come with me. Stacy had come over and I asked her if she'd drive me to the hospital to see my mom. She didn't think it was a good idea, seeing that my mom was sick, but I insisted saying, "Well, I just want to see her and tell her what happened."

The old man must have heard this because he very softly asked me to come down to his room; that he wanted to talk to me. I thought he might be wanting to make amends and said okay. He made some angry remarks while following me down to his room and I kept thinking he would try and push me down the stairs. I'd seen him do it several times to my mom. I was nervous and ready to jump down the stairwell if he made a move at me. He didn't. We went into his room and I noticed a bottle of rum. I picked it up, took a swallow and held the bottle just in case. "Put that bottle down!" he yelled. I just took another drink and held onto it. He was getting angrier all the time and finally took a swing at me. He missed, hit his camera which was on a tripod and broke some of his photographic equipment. This threw him into a rage and he came at me. I broke the bottom of the bottle off on his table and said, "Okay, lets have a fight!" He stopped, still raging, and yelled, "Some day I'm going to shoot you!" "You'd better be quick about it," I told him, "because I'm preparing to do the same thing to you."

He took another poke at me, then chased me halfway up the stairs screaming for me to come back. I ran out, grabbed my suitcase and went to the car. Joan and Gord followed, still crying. I was almost crying too as Stacy drove us over to the hospital. It was after visiting hours but the nurse could see we were all upset and asked us to wait. Then they wheeled her out onto this porch and we started telling her what happened. "I'll kick the old man out!" she said at first. "No. It's okay," I said. I'll just move out. I still have my job at the Tomahawk, so don't worry." "Where will you live?" she asked. "I think I'll move in with Ray," I replied. She was upset on hearing this but didn't say too much.

I guess we talked for almost an hour. After a while we were all crying and my mom was trying to calm us down. It'd been a long time — since I was about thirteen — that I'd cried like that. Something just broke loose inside me and I felt upset about everything. Then the nurse came in and told us we'd have to leave. Mom was just saying how she would get a court injunction to kick the old man out of the house. "Take it easy," I told her. "I'll be all right. You just stay in the hospital till you're better. There's plenty of time to deal with the old man."

The nurse gave her a sedative and we left. Stacy dropped Joan and Gord off at Rog's place then took me over to Ray's. I walked into his place with my bags, sat down in a big chair and started looking through some book and thinking about how I was going to approach things with Ray. When he came in a little later he found me sitting there reading and looking like I'd lived there all my life. "Are you moving in?" he asked. I said "Yeah" and he asked me what happened. So I told him the whole story about being kicked out by the old man. He just said "Okay" and didn't ask any more questions.

Ray was still at VCC doing his second year of college. He was sharing this basement with a US Army deserter while Gordie and Gerri Andrew and their little boy Keith lived upstairs. There were two rooms in the basement and I stayed there just like one of the guys. It wasn't until sometime later that Ray and I started having serious sexual relations.

About a week later, in early November, Stacy came over

to the Tomahawk and asked me if I'd fill in for her at work because she and Sue Thom were going down to Seattle for the weekend. She had just gotten this job at a nightclub on Davie Street near Burrard called the Elegant Parlour. So I said, "Sure," and worked there the next Friday and Saturday. When Stacy came back the owner, a guy everybody called "Pop," said he wouldn't take her on again. "Bobbi, you're hired, she's not. I need reliable girls." When I told Stacy she just laughed and said, "That's okay, I didn't want the job anyway."

So I quit my job at the Tomahawk and started working weekends at the Elegant. The pay was pretty good: $140 a month plus about $10 a night in tips — enough to live on. As far as waitressing goes, it wasn't a bad job. The place opened early in the evening and closed at 3 or 4 in the morning. Most of the patrons were Blacks, some up from Seattle and others from Vancouver. Then there were the usual pimps, prostitutes and so forth. A bunch of people who later formed the V-Bag or Vancouver Black Action Group used to hang around the Elegant quite a bit and the Black guy who shared the basement with us, Darrell, introduced us to a lot of his friends in this group. The Panthers used to come up for the weekend. They would rent fancy places on Denman — the Oceanside and other West End hotels — and come down to the Elegant at night. They'd buy themselves a hooker and that kind of a crap. Most of them came on pretty strong, wearing their Black uniforms and caps, a lot of buttons, and trying to look as mean as possible. It was almost theatrical. Co-captain Curtis Harris was a real "rounder" type, but another co-captain named Aaron Dixon seemed an okay guy. He was at least quiet and polite and dressed in normal clothes at the club. He was a friend of Pops who was always giving money to the Panthers. Pops was pretty strange; a short guy who looked after the door. People didn't even know he owned the place. In fact, I didn't know either till the second week; I'd just thought he was the doorman. Anyway, this Pops and Aaron Dixon used to have talks in this little room.

At first this heavy Panther line and fancy dress turned me off — especially when I saw them drinking and picking up hookers and learned that they were living high in rooms overlooking English Bay. It sort of reminded me of the NARP people, drinking all the time and yet talking big about politics. I felt the conflict, but didn't give it much thought at the time. I just couldn't take their politics very seriously, though this didn't bother me because I wasn't really political myself.

They had a real crazy bouncer named Eddie at the club. Whenever he bounced someone he would beat the holy hell out of him. I remember one time when he got a notion to pick me up and carry me around the club. I was really surprised at first; this big lug holding me up over his head by my legs and neck. A lot of people were looking at us and laughing. I got angry and reached down and gashed his face with my fingernails. When he dropped me I ran to the kitchen and grabbed a big knife, preparing to stab him if he tried anything else. They fired him that night — but hired him back the next weekend. Pops was always doing that — firing the guy for doing something stupid, then rehiring him. I thought it must have been hard to get good bouncers.

Ray quit school at the end of the semester, around mid-December. He'd been getting $85 a month from the Indian Affairs Department plus books and school fees. In NARP we were working on a newsletter, doing work on skid row and

157

staging a few demonstrations. NARP politics at that time were pretty much patterned after the programs of the Panther Party. But in fact, conditions among Indians were quite different than among Blacks and it was really hard to mobilize Indians around political issues. We had a bit more success with work on skid row — but it was much like social work without much politics. We had a hall downtown and we'd do things like sober up drunk Indians and send them home. There was always a lot of singing and stuff going on — kind of like missionary work. We had some political discussions with Indians who'd just come in off the reserves, but this was difficult with down-and-outers and drunks. Jerry Jones was a craftsman and got a group going doing leatherwork ... it was all stuff like that. Ray was getting more and more demoralized about NARP politics and I was losing interest. Both of us started thinking that what we were into wasn't going anywhere — it was more like welfare work than radical politics, but at the time I didn't have any great interest in radical politics either.

When I'd started going to all these NARP meetings, discussions and so on it was like entering a new world for me. At first I thought most of these people were crazy, talking about revolution, socialism, Marxism, communism, "offing the pigs" and so on. The more leftists I met, Gordie Andrew and Ray's friends, the more it seemed to me they were all alike. I met Trotskyists, old CPers, Internationalists, PWM members and they all seemed the same, just with varying degrees of enthusiasm. At first I felt I was being bombarded by all their talk; that I was going to get sucked into this great wave of whatever it was they were doing. I resisted this for a long time, always arguing with Ray who would categorically defend the Canadian working class. I didn't like white people, and we'd argue about that too. About the only thing we agreed on was being against wholesale integration, though we had different reasons. I would say, "It's not possible anyway. Even if we wanted to integrate we couldn't, because these people don't want us."

Ray would usually end up calling me a racist and I would say "Fuck off!" Then he got on to me about my swearing so much. It had never occurred to me before that I swore a lot; our whole family used to swear and all the people I grew up with were fishermen's kids from Steveston docks and they all swore like it was just the natural way of talking. So I never thought about it one way or another. At first Ray said it wasn't ladylike. But that just made me laugh. I would go into theatrics saying, "Oh pardon me, Sir." He'd respond to my making fun of him by saying I was ignorant. And I'd say, "Well, I'm just an ignorant person, what're you gonna do?" So it went on like this, us arguing back and forth and getting nowhere.

Another thing that bugged me about Ray was that he didn't want me reading his books. I don't know why. Guess he was sort of possessive about his books. He gave me a copy of Fanon's *Black Skin, White Mask* and said I should buy my own books if I wanted to start reading. This just irritated me and I'd pick up one of his books anyway, saying, "If you don't like it, just try and stop me!" He got mad and said I had no respect for his personal property.

After reading the Fanon book, which didn't impress me too much at the time, I picked up *Quotations from Chairman Mao* and read a few things. I just couldn't understand what he meant by talking about a "democratic dictatorship of the proletariat." "How could a dictatorship be democratic?" I thought. By this time I never asked Ray any questions; he would just give me an answer I couldn't accept or understand, then we'd start arguing and I'd end up swearing at

159

him and he'd tell me not to swear, and so on. So I stopped asking him things after a while. When I asked Gerri she explained that in our society the bourgeoisie dictated to the masses, but that in a socialist society it was the masses of workers and peasants who dictated to the bourgeoisie. This made a bit more sense to me than what I'd heard others say.

Ray was just beginning to read some Marx and he would say to me that if I really wanted to understand the system I'd have to read Marx. I'd just say, "I don't want to read what some German honkie had to say a hundred years ago!" "Don't categorize people like that," Ray would say, "it's racist." "Fuck you!" I'd reply. "They're all a bunch of honkies! It's working class kids that've kicked my ass all my life!" Ray would just keep saying that I was a racist and being subjective. And I guess I was. Somehow, I felt ignorant and isolated. And I guess I was. I was being bombarded by all these people who seemed able to discuss everything intelligently and calmly — socialism, the rottenness of capitalist society, "Third World" struggles, and so on. And while all this stuff was raining down on me I was just trying to find definitions which made some sense to me. I didn't understand much of what I read, just bits and pieces. I couldn't seem to grasp the totality of it — you know, what socialism and revolution were all about. And meanwhile, I felt like I was being sucked into this thing I didn't understand.

Another problem I had was relating to people on a human level — just being decent to them, including Ray. I had to go through a lot of difficulties and changes in this area just to be able to relate to people and work with them. I hadn't begun to get over the dehumanizing effects of my Toronto experience. At first, most of the NARP people didn't like me — especially Gerri and Sue. They couldn't stand me, and only put up with me at all because we had NARP politics in common. I was frank to the point that it was painful, and sometimes I was pretty inconsiderate or plain obnoxious. I never wasted any words or hesitated in saying what was on my mind. Despite my political ignorance — or perhaps because of it — I was pretty aggressive and arrogant.

NARP at this time was also faced with a big contradiction. Most NARP people were students or ex-students and they'd have all these intellectual discussions which didn't have much meaning in terms of what they were doing. Like they'd talk about Vietnam, US imperialism, Soviet revisionism, but it didn't coincide with their practice. And like much of the Left at that time, they never bothered about relating questions of theory and strategy to their practice. It was really issue-oriented and there wasn't much concern with long-range planning or developing and carrying out the struggle in a consistent way.

The few actions we carried out got a lot of media attention, inflating the importance of what we were doing and staving off the demoralization which most people felt. Ray was speaking a lot at universities and reporters would come around asking us for interviews. Sometimes we were even interviewed on television. I think the media sensationalism and play-up of NARP had to do with our picking up on the Panther line, just changing Black Power into Red Power. Anyway, it wasn't because of our numbers or real strength. Actually, we were still only a very small group: Gerri and Gordie, Ray and me, Hank Mack, Sue Thom and Dave Cuthand. Maybe ten or twelve other people, like my sister Joan, Jerry Jones and Pauline Jones, were on the periphery. And even with this small number, there were several trends developing. Sue was moving in a religious direction — that is, into traditional religion. The Big House dancing societies on the West Coast were still operating and a few of them were undergoing a real revival. For a great many years these Big Houses had been sustained by a small number of people on each reserve, those who kept alive the traditional dancing and religion. Now, however, lots of young people were going into the Big Houses and Sue was seriously thinking of doing it herself.

Gerri was getting caught up in one aspect of Indian oppression and losing sight of the overall struggle. She was real concerned about the social aspects of racism — how it affected Indians in education, for example, or in the job market. Ray, on the other hand, was doing a lot of thinking about what was necessary in a revolutionary struggle. He was really confused about the whole question of armed struggle in relation to other forms of revolutionary struggle.

Then there was the antagonism between Gordie, who was white and the rest of us. It seemed that Gordie's ideas were always accepted without question, maybe because he could always argue them on the basis of "Marxism-Leninism." I noticed this right away and some of us felt almost incompetent around him and started resenting his presence — particularly Ray and me. Gord and Ray were constantly at each other's throats and after a while it got pretty bad.

The whole period of about a month in December of 1968, when a lot of actions related to the Mohawk blockade of the border crossing in the East were going on, NARP was seething with these different tendencies and contradictions. But they weren't openly discussed; people were afraid or inhibited about bringing up our differences because everyone was affected personally. And it seemed especially hard to bring things into the open because of Gordie's presence.

Despite his claims about being a Marxist, every time someone would say, "Well, let's try and deal with the question of how you make revolution," he'd put a brake on the discussion saying that these things take a long time, that a lot more development would have to take place and so on. And we believed him, at least I did — thinking that the answer would just come to us someday from the sky or something; that we just weren't ready to understand things like how you went about making revolution.

This came at about the peak of the Mohawk blockade. Their reserve, the St. Regis Reserve, is split in half — part on the US side and part in Canada. The closest store was on the American side, but they kept being harassed by Customs every time they crossed the border with supplies. The nearest Canadian store was some ten miles from the Reserve. Anyway, they protested Government's violation of their treaty rights by blocking the border bridge on Cornwall Island which is on the St. Regis Reserve. It was getting critical, with a real threat of police violence, so we organized a support demonstration in Vancouver. Ray did most of the organizing work, phoning around and talking to people. We had a big meeting at the Indian Centre and the next day a demonstration was held and fifty or sixty Indians showed up at the courthouse. Ben and Phillip Paul and Hank were the speakers and they all said pretty much the same thing — about how treaty and aboriginal rights were being violated by the colonial bureaucracy of the Indian Affairs Department. There was also a lot of rhetoric about Government injustices toward Indians, especially by this Phillip Paul, who later became head of the Land Claims Research for the Union of B.C. Chiefs — one of the big organizations which represents Indians legally as far as the government is concerned.

Anyway, we were all pretty pleased with the demonstration; and about how quickly and well Ray had been able to organize it over the phone. And the Mohawks on Cornwall Island did get the treaty rights for their reserve recognized by the government, even though about fifty of their members were arrested on minor charges related to blockading the border crossing.

Soon after the demonstration the problem with Gordie came up again, especially in conversations between Hank, Ray and me. Gordie kept saying that systematic study wasn't necessary, that we had a program and should just get busy on it. Because he was hanging us up on this question, we thought it would be best for the organization if Gordie left. Hank backed down, however, saying "It would be embarrassing. Might hurt his feelings," and things like that. Ray and I didn't have the courage to bring it out into the open without Hank's support, knowing that Doug and Sue — to say nothing of Gerri — were pretty close to Gordie on a personal level and wouldn't do anything that might hurt a friend. It was that kind of group; people were really more concerned about friendships than they were about the political consequences of our practice.

Ray was getting pretty demoralized. I didn't really understand the difference between Gordie's political thinking and Ray's. The only thing I could see was that we needed to have some long-range plan. Like most of the time there'd be a flurry of activity, then nothing for a long time, than another flurry. It was sort of frustrating. We were mainly waiting, then reacting to things as they happened. In January 1969 for example when this North Vancouver judge named Mahon said in court that he was going to teach these Indians a lesson because they were stealing so much, we did some investigating in the court records and then held a courthouse demonstration. This Judge Mahon sentenced this guy named Naheny to two years in prison for some minor theft, saying that he would make an example of him for other Indians. At our demonstration we demanded a public apology from Mahon as well as a government guarantee that he wouldn't try any more cases involving Indians because he was a racist.

A lot of Indians came out to the demonstration, including all the Nahenys. There were also a large number of police, especially plainclothesmen. They took pictures of everyone as we marched around. The courthouse was in the police building just across from the hospital on 13th Avenue in North Vancouver. It lasted about an hour and it was the first time I'd done any public speaking. Everybody warned me not to swear, to try and control myself. And, in fact, I was quite pleased with myself for getting through almost a half-hour without swearing — even though before the demonstration I'd just say "Fuck off!" whenever somebody mentioned my not swearing. I didn't mind not swearing, but I minded people telling me not to. Whenever people said I swore too much I'd get indignant and resist by saying, "Oh, fuck off! I'll swear as much as I want to. I don't claim to be some sort of 'lady' and your moral arguments against swearing are just stupid. So just leave me alone!"

During my talk I said we didn't want racist judges like this Mahon trying Indians; that Naheny should get a retrial because he didn't get a fair trial and the sentence was ridiculous; and Indians were forced to steal in the first place because they were oppressed, couldn't get jobs and so forth.

There were some other NARP actions in early 1969, but they weren't usually well thought out or very effective. The Indian people just weren't that politically conscious. They wanted to do something, to be active in some way, but most of their energies went into strictly cultural-nationalist things — like wearing headbands and beads or refusing to speak English. Most of our program didn't work because of this — though we did do some good research into the Indian community, found out what was really going on, whether people actually wanted to become berry-pickers and stuff like that. But it was difficult for us to work our any practical, workable programs because there simply wasn't a hell of a lot you could do. Every time we started an action program we were stopped by the apathy of the people.

I was still working weekends at the Elegant and Ray started looking for a job instead of going back to school. In January we found a place near Carroll and Hastings Street in downtown Vancouver and started actually living together — having sexual relations. We lived practically in the heart of skid row and I got to know something of the people and life down there. I drifted around, talking to people and trying to find out why they were there, what they were doing and so on. Most were transient, except for a few of the older people. I talked a lot with a kindly fellow named Mike Rufus. He had very long hair and was always drunk and beat up.

Living with Ray like this hadn't changed my mind about getting married, having kids. I was still afraid of getting caught up in anything really permanent. It seemed like such a waste of time. Most people I knew ended up with their marriages on the rocks, and Ray and I were still arguing about politics and other things. I just sort of drifted into the relationship with Ray, same as I had with the two other guys I'd lived with, though I liked and respected Ray a bit more.

Being in NARP hadn't really affected my character very much. I was still really irresponsible — just took things pretty well as they came and if they ended well, then okay.

I never put any real effort into anything, particularly any emotional effort. I hadn't yet taken myself to task — been very self-critical; just floated along more or less with whatever was happening.

In February NARP activities really slowed down. Ray and I would talk, but even our discussions were very superficial. I kept busy selling newsletters, answering mail and so forth. I also started doing some reading, but this meant spending most of my time looking up words in the dictionary. My English was still pretty horrible and I was incredibly confused and politically ignorant. I didn't know what I wanted to do with the rest of my life and sometimes Ray and I talked about this. My relations with people were still bad, and that's the main reason we moved out of the Andrew's basement. Gerri and I didn't get along well for a number of reasons. Sometimes I was just plain obnoxious with her. For instance, if she or someone else said something I didn't like, I'd get smart with them, make some wisecrack and not discuss things seriously or on a rational level. I was very subjective most of the time and Gerri didn't like it. She was a very soft-spoken and reasonable person; her whole manner and carriage was different than mine. But then, she was really concerned about personal relationships, which I wasn't. Anyway, she and Gordie ended up asking me and Ray to move out of their basement.

At this time we had a hall down on Carroll St. and carried out some activities such as maintaining a street patrol around skid row to protect Indians against police harassment. It was pretty missionary-oriented, however, with most of our time being spent taking drunks off the street, caring for the down-and-outers, trying to prevent people from being arrested and so forth. We also had what were called "educationals," as well as social gatherings with singing and that sort of thing. But it wasn't very political and wasn't paying for itself. The money was coming out of our own pockets and the whole thing wasn't really productive. The PWM asked if they could put their press in the back and we said it was okay. They agreed to pay part of the rent.

Around the end of February Ray and I were talking a lot about what we were doing, whether we wanted to leave and so on. A big problem was that neither of us really wanted to admit that we wanted Gordie out of NARP mainly because he was white. I think we had doubts whether, as Indians we could do anything better on our own; and we resented feeling like this. In any event, we were sort of afraid to discuss that aspect of it and so avoided talking about why we really wanted Gordie out. The contradictions just kept building and we became supremely frustrated and demoralized.

Out of the City

Then one Sunday morning I came home from work tired and feeling down. Ray had been drinking and was really depressed. "I'm sick of Vancouver," he said. "Sick of Gordie and sick of Indian politics. I just want to split; get out of Vancouver. My dad wrote from Ashcroft and asked me to come up there and work with him on the railroad. I think I'll do it. You can come along if you want."

I thought that maybe he didn't want me to come. "Well, if you want me to come I'll come," I said. "And if you don't I'll stay." I told him it sounded as if he didn't really want me to go with him. "Oh no," he said, "I didn't mean it like that. It's just that if you don't want to go to Ashcroft with me ... well, I can understand why — there's not much up there except my folks and a job for me with the Canadian Pacific Railway."

The next day, on the 1st of March, we set out hitch-hiking for Ashcroft. We got some real short rides and it seemed to take forever just to get out of Vancouver. It was almost like walking the first thirty miles. Finally we got to a place called Mission City and then got a ride straight to Agassiz. From there we had to walk a few miles to the Trans-Canada Highway. It was really cold, snow all over the ground, and we were lucky to catch a ride all the way to Ashcroft, which was about three miles off the main highway. We'd left at 6 a.m. and didn't get to Ashcroft until after 4 in the afternoon. The whole trip had been about 250 miles.

Ray's parents had moved up to Ashcroft from Agassiz a couple of months earlier and Sue Thom moved in with them.

It was the first time I'd met Ray's folks and they both seemed pretty nice. There was also this strange little cocker spaniel named Donovan. Ray's dad, Bill, was a section foreman for CPR and they provided a house for the family. It wasn't a very fancy place. There was no central heating or hot running water. We had to use big quilts at night to keep warm in the freezing bedrooms upstairs.

I had decided to keep my job at the Elegant, hitch-hiking down on Friday and working the weekends. I didn't know how long we, or I, would be staying there in Ashcroft and thought it best to hold onto my job for at least a couple of months.

In the morning at 7 a.m., Marion, Ray's mom, woke us up. I remember thinking how different Bill was from the night before when he'd been so polite and soft-spoken. He seemed just like a big spoiled kid in the morning. Marion brought his shoes and socks and overboots and he was tramping around the house throwing tantrums and yelling, "Why isn't this ready? Why isn't that ready?" Sometimes Marion picked up a broom and whacked him a couple of times, telling him not to be so cranky. Then he'd walk around sheepishly for a while like a kid who'd been naughty. I found this very funny and had a good laugh at the whole scene. After breakfast Ray and Bill took off for work, returning about 4 p.m.

There was no reserve in the town of Ashcroft where our CPR house was. A few Indians lived in the town, but most lived on the reserve which was about two miles west of the town near the highway. The Ashcroft Reserve actually covered quite a bit more land than that, but it was all leased out to cattle ranchers. This had all happened since 1958, when Chief Kirkpatrick started leasing out miles and miles of Indian land. Only one small hill opposite the row of houses was kept by the band for some religious or super-stitious reasons. There were some old foxes living there which the people believed watched over them.

The people here were Thompson Indians of the Cook's Ferry band. Another reserve was not far away in the Highland Valley where Bethlehem Copper had what was supposed to be one of the richest copper mines in the country. Along a road that ran behind our CPR house one would come to Highland Valley and then to another reserve some thirteen miles from the house. About eighty people lived in Ashcroft Reserve and another fifty or so up in Highland Valley. Many of these Indians were mixed bloods — part white or Chinese and part Indian — and the town Indians were mostly half-breeds. Further up in the Highland lived an old lady, her daughters and a bunch of her grandchildren — about fifteen in all. The daughters bounced back and forth between Ashcroft, Kamloops, Cache Creek and their home, leaving the old lady to raise the children.

One afternoon during my first week in Ashcroft, Ray and I and Donovan went for a walk up into the hills. It was early spring and the cactus plants were just coming out. They had little green needles which were stiff and sunk into your skin pretty good. Well, I had just climbed over this fence enclosing some ranch and we were all running down the hill when I slipped and brought my hands down right on this bunch of cactus. The needles had cut through three of my fingers in various directions, pinning them together. I felt a dull, numbing pain and got a bit scared. I kept telling Ray, "Pull 'em out! Pull 'em out!" He said, "Let's go back to the house and let mom do it. She knows about these things. Those needles have little barbs and if you take them out wrong you'll just tear your skin."

Back at the house we couldn't find Marion: she was out washing clothes or something. I asked Bill to help but he almost got sick just looking at the mess. Sue refused also, just kept moaning "Ohoo, ohoo." But feeling sorry for me didn't help. I was getting kind of faint and the pain was getting worst. I tried to pull some out, but that just made it more painful. Finally Ray came in with Marion. She gently and very slowly started taking them out — I still don't know how. It took quite a long time, then she had me soak my had in something. Next she took care of Donovan, who'd also picked up some needles in his paws. I felt okay in a couple of hours.

A few days later I met some friends of Sue's. One of them a guy named Sid Libidoff, was a Ukrainian who'd been adopted by the Lewis family. I think this happened quite a lot — Indian families adopting white kids. One of Ray's uncles was Irish; he'd been adopted by the Thoms when he was very young. Anyway, I liked this Sid quite a bit. He was real easy-going and we talked with him a lot, explaining about NARP and how we'd come up to Ashcroft to get away from the city for a while and try to pull ourselves together. Sue was reading Mao Tse-tung at the time and we had a lot of political discussions and arguments. Ray was really anti-Mao — I guess it was a holdover from his involvement with the Trotskyists. Anyway, we all read and discussed Mao's *Little Red Book*. We found it pretty exciting, especially Sue and I, thinking these quotations from Chairman Mao were all we needed. I guess we picked up on this idea from the Panthers, who used a lot of Mao's quotations all the time.

After a while, however, we decided that reading the red

book wasn't really like studying Marxism-Leninism. It helped if you already had a theory, strategy and practice but otherwise it didn't get you much beyond a superficial knowledge and politics. The discussions were good, nevertheless, and we learned quite a bit talking to Sid and different people around Ashcroft.

Bill Thom was a heavy drinker and every weekend he'd get sloshed right out of his head. A couple of weeks after we got there, on a Friday night (Donna was filling in for me at the Elegant), the chief and his family came over. Usually on a reserve, you know, a person becomes chief because nobody else has the crass to run for the office — mainly because the chief is completely under the thumb of the Indian Agent. So generally these chiefs are lazy do-nothings. They tend to be the lowest and most opportunistic people on the reserve; people who don't want to do any work, just get something for nothing by being yes-men for the Indian Agents.

Anyway, this Chief Kirkpatrick, his wife Sarah and their son and daughter-in-law, Pearl, came over to the house. It was already pretty late and all of them but Pearl were drunk. She was a few months pregnant but still pretty slim; the others were all fat and heavy. Ray and I were sleeping upstairs when I heard some noise and went downstairs after throwing on my jeans and sweater. The chief and his son were fighting, really going at it. Bill was watching. Then this Sarah starts screaming at Pearl, saying the baby wasn't her son's, who was in jail when she got pregnant. I thought Pearl was a really decent person and didn't believe the old lady. I couldn't figure out, though, what she was doing with this guy anyway; he was completely nuts. The only thing was that all the men in the Reserve seemed to be not a hell of a lot different. They'd work for a while, then quit, stay drunk for a few weeks, then got back to work. It just seemed to continue like that.

Well, these two big guys were fighting and I was just standing there watching. Then all of a sudden the son hits his old man and he falls back against me, bashing me against the stove and giving me a nice gash on my leg. Without even thinking I give him a big shove with my feet and he landed face-first on the floor. He was real drunk, couldn't even stand up without a lot of effort. Realizing what I'd done I thought, "Oh, Christ, he's going to try and kill me now." He'd struggled to his feet and was coming at me. I grabbed onto his fists and kept him back. Fortunately, he was so drunk he couldn't even see me at three feet; his eyes were kind of rolling around as he tried to get a bead on me. I was really scared; he was just about to pin me up against one of the walls. Then Bill stepped in, spun the chief around and pushed him out the door. Out in the cold night air the guy passed clean out.

Inside the house Sarah had started slapping Pearl around, really hitting and kicking her. Sue had come down a while earlier and she tried to stop the old lady. She was so big, however, that we couldn't seem to get her out the door. Marion was just standing there rolling cigarettes — she's a chain-smoker — getting madder all the time. She didn't get mad often, but when she did, phew, the energy she'd stored up just came out all at once. Finally, she shouted, "Sarah! What are you doing?" She'd burst in like lighting, grabbed the woman by the scruff of her neck and ran out the door with her. Marion had gotten up such a speed that Sarah plunged up against the old stove that was standing at the back of the porch.

So the whole family except Pearl was laying helter-skelter, all over the place. Bill knew they'd wake up soon, start drinking again and continue the ruckus. We decided to pile them into their truck and have Pearl drive them home. But Pearl didn't drive. She started waking up her husband so he could take them home, but when he woke up he asked, "Who hit me?" He still couldn't really see very well. Bill said, "I hit you! And I'll hit you again if you don't take your father home!" He looked at the chief and asked, "Who hit my father?" "I hit him too," said Bill, "and I'll do it again if you don't get home!" Well, the son was kind of worried. Bill was a real big man, much taller than Ray, and he'd been a wrestler in his younger days and had worked hard for many years on the railroad.

The chief was just coming around and they were about to take off in the truck when the fighting started all over again. We just watched for a minute, then went inside and locked the doors.

After that incident the Kirkpatrick boys — and there were a bunch of them — used to ride around the CPR house and hurl insults at us, trying to be intimidating. We just ignored them. They all seemed a bit nuts. The court had indicted them because they'd been pulled in on drunk charges so many times. No one in the family was allowed to drink, but they'd get others to buy booze for them so it didn't matter much. The chief never came back to Bill's house as long as I was there.

Whenever we went out hiking, Donovan came along. He was quite a character. Once we were walking and came across this rabbit. We decided to try to catch it and for about an hour Ray and I were chasing all over the place trying to tire him out. Finally we got him in a corner, between some big rocks. Then, all of a sudden, Donovan charges in and starts barking. The rabbit, panicked into a burst of energy, bounded about four feet in the air and was off again. The last we saw of him he was darting into his hole.

We did a lot of things like that during the first month or so. There were plenty of hills and caves in Ashcroft and it was fun just hiking around and exploring. A couple of times I called Donna and she would work the whole weekend for me at the Elegant. A few times we went snake hunting and Marion and I would often go on walks while the men were working. It was kind of nice living out of the city, being away from the crowds and narrow social work that had become NARP politics.

In May I got pregnant with our first kid, Tania. Both Ray and I had kind of wanted a kid, though I still had plenty of reservations. We realized that if I went ahead and had it we'd both have to become more stable and responsible people. Then one Sunday, after I'd gotten off work, I went over to visit my mom and found Joan there, all upset and in tears. She said she was pregnant and didn't want to tell mom. She asked me what she should do, whether she should get an abortion or what. She was still just a kid herself and was very scared and worried. My first reaction was anger at this Jerry Jones for getting her pregnant and then buggering off. He was a useless sort anyway.

I asked Joan to come up to Ashcroft with me. Ray and I had been thinking of moving out on our own and she could stay with us for a time. We'd bought this '57 Rambler a few weeks earlier and I drove back to Ashcroft with Joan. It was Sunday night when we finally got to the house. I noticed that Ray, Bill, Sid and Joey Hewitt were standing outside and thought that maybe something was wrong. Ray was standing there looking real mad so I said to Joan, "Stay in the car. I'll be right back. And lock the doors!" Ray didn't get mad very easily, so I knew something really had to be wrong for him to have that look in his eye. Bill was obviously very drunk. When I walked up to them Bill said, "Where the hell you been all this time? What d'ya mean getting home so late? It's damn near midnight!"

Then, before I could say anything, Ray shouts, "Well, that's fucking enough! Just leave Bobbi out of this!" They argued back and forth for a time, then Bill said, "Well, just pack up your things and get out!" "That's fine with me," Ray replied.

He came over to me and said, "We'd better go, Bobbi. Get in the car." I went around the other side to get in just as Bill says, "Hey, Ray." And when Ray said, "What?" and turned around, Bill hauled off and hit him. Next thing you know there was a big fight with the two of them rolling around on the ground. Ray was strong as a bull when he got mad and the old man was pretty drunk. After Ray beat up on him pretty good we got into the car and left. Funniest thing was that Ray turned to Joey and said, "You know, I've been wanting to do that for years."

Apparently, earlier in the evening, Bill had gone into Sue's room and found her with these two guys, Sid and Timmy. They'd just been talking but the old man accused Sue of doing all kinds of immoral things and threw the guys out. Sid didn't say anything, but Timmy mouthed off and Bill knocked him around a bit and then began insulting and threatening Sue. Ray intervened and told him he shouldn't do it. That's when the argument between Bill and Ray started. Being a big guy, Bill terrorized everybody in the family when he was drunk — he also got pretty foul-mouthed and obnoxious with the women, pawing them and things. I couldn't stand it and used to tell him, "Just fuck off! Keep your hands off me or I'll kill you!" As time went on I started being generally mean to the old man and this used to bug Ray. He'd tell me his dad was harmless and that I should be a bit nicer to him. I'd tell him, "Look, if you teach your old man some manners, I'll be nice to him."

After the fight we drove down to Vancouver with Sid, Joey and this girl named Shirley. We stayed at my mom's and Ray phoned Sue and told her to call in sick for him at work, saying he'd be out for two days. Of course Bill, the foreman, knew it wasn't true, but he wasn't about to fire his son. On Tuesday we drove back up, getting there by mid-afternoon and having to look for a place to stay. Joan had stayed with mom in Vancouver after telling her she was pregnant and wanted to have the kid. We drove the others home and then spent the night in our Rambler, folding the seats back into a bed. Sid had asked us to stay with him, but I didn't want to. He was a real nice guy, but was always drinking: he never flipped out or anything, but he was drunk all the time. Ray only drank on weekends.

It was the first time I'd spent a night in a car like this and Ray and I laughed about it for a long time. Next day we drove over to Cache Creek, about five miles north on the highway, and checked into this ranch-like place called the Semlin Motel. We got a little cabin and one bedroom, which was joined to other cabins by common walls. Unfortunately, we had a real crazy white guy living next door.

On weekends Ray, Sid and Joey would go drink at the pubs. They all knew I was under age because I'd mouthed off once to one of the owners and he'd asked to see my ID. It didn't bother me. I'd go visit Sue whenever they went drinking; Ray would drive me over and pick me up when they were finished. Ray and his dad had gotten back on more or less good terms and sometimes the guys would go over and drink with Bill and Marion. Sue and I spent most of our time outside just talking about politics and other things. In May the weather really starts turning warm and by June it's hot as hell.

It was around this time when there was a big brawl in the pub of the old Ashcroft Hotel. The day before, the police had stopped Ray, Sue and me. They focused in on Ray and one of them said, "Look, we know who you are and we don't want any trouble around here. No Red Power or any of that kind of shit!" They were really rude and tried to intimidate all three of us. They asked Sue and me what our names were and then asked sarcastically, "What? Are both of you this guy's wives?" We didn't answer and they drove off laughing.

Then Ray went into the pub and met Sid and Joey. They were talking about Red Power and New Democratic Party (NDP) politics with this Cliff Hartley, the son of the NDP Member of Parliament for the area. They got into an argument when Ray said the NDP was just a reformist party and Cliff was maintaining it was socialist. The argument got a little loud and the bartender came over and told Ray to leave. Cliff said, "Hey, how come just Ray has to leave? We were both arguing!" The bartender just said, "OK, you can fuck off too." Cliff got pretty angry and replied, "You'd better watch out who you're talking to." Then another bartender came over and they grabbed Ray and started to throw him out. "Just put me down," Ray said, "I can walk out by myself!" Then for no apparent reason, the bartenders started beating up on Ray. Sid and Joey got into it and before long most of the people in the pub were fighting and soon it spilled out onto the street. I was sitting with Sue just across from the hotel at the Thom's place. I walked across after a while, wondering where Ray was and what had happened. Sue and I looked inside the pub and saw these four bartenders beating up on Ray. They were keeping him in the

179

pub while he was trying to get out. He was close to the door and a couple of friends were trying to put him out. It was crazy. Sue ran in the back, grabbed a pool cue and started jabbing the guy who was doing the most of the holding in the small of his back. Finally he let go and Ray was able to get out.

We held a meeting that night and everybody wanted to boycott the Ashcroft Hotel and have a demonstration. We agreed, held a few more meetings and called a demonstration in the town. Just about everybody came — must have been over fifty people. Newspaper reporters were buzzing around talking to everybody they could corner. Ray and Cliff spoke at the demonstration and then did interviews with the press. They told what had happened at the hotel, said it demonstrated that the owner was clearly a racist and asked people to boycott the place. The response of the owner was to bar a whole bunch of Indians from the pub for life. It didn't matter to them, as there was another pub just down the street. Ray and Sid, however, were barred from both pubs and had to do their drinking after that in Cache Creek. The boycott was fairly effective, though, for a time. And people as far off as Kamloops respected it.

A couple of days later some guy from Kamloops, about fifty miles east of Cache Creek, told us they were having an education symposium at the Canadian Inn but that none of the students from Kamloops were allowed to attend. Five of them had gone in anyway and the priest running their parochial residential school had threatened to fail them. We decided to go up and talk to the students. They told us that this Catholic school was the only residential or boarding school in the whole Kamloops District and drew students from as far away as Chase and Spences Bridge. Kamloops itself had one of the largest Shuswap bands in the area. So the students were from various bands and their families lived as far as fifty or sixty miles away. The priest had a strict policy of keeping the students on the school grounds. Those with parents in the Kamloops Reserve could go home in the evenings, and then they'd be driven directly there by the teachers. Students who had parents outside Kamloops Reserve couldn't leave the school grounds at all ... not even if they had other close relatives in the town or Reserve. The only way they could get away from the school was for their mother or father to pick them up. These students wanted to go to the education symposium to complain about these and other school restrictions. They also wanted to protest the symposium fee of $35 a day, which even the chiefs couldn't afford to pay. The only exceptions were for a small number of students chosen by the Department's Indian Agents, and none of these were from Kamloops.

After hearing this we decided to picket the symposium and demand that they take off the $35 a day fee and allow local Indians to attend. Quite a few people joined us and we demonstrated and picketed all day. Sue Thom was the spokesman. She told reporters that if the fee was removed for Indians who didn't have the money, and this was announced on radio and TV, we'd go home. She told them it was a joke to have a symposium on Indian education and have only two Indians participating. One was an MP from Ottawa and the other a chief from up north. The first day the whole audience except for these two and a few chosen Indian students was white ... liberal professors and so forth.

By the end of the day they said they were willing to drop the fees, and for the next two days about 200 Indians attended. They came from all over the area and insisted on participating in discussions about procedures and so on. Pretty soon the whites drifted away and none would attend the third day's meetings. It was funny. This Len Marchand, an Indian MP and Special Assistant to Minister of Education, couldn't find anything to say to an audience of ordinary Indians. He was real good talking to white liberals but couldn't talk with the just the average Indians. The head of the symposium, a professor from UBC, got so perturbed about Indians wanting to participate, that he closed the symposium without their having passed any of their resolutions on Indian education.

In mid-May I quit my job at the Elegant Parlour. Sue, Marion and I got a job weeding a potato farm about a mile from Ashcroft. The owner asked us what we'd charge to weed the whole field. We figured it would take us five or six days so told him we would take $150 for the job. He agreed and we started working the next day. In three days we were halfway through, but then it rained — which was really unusual for Ashcroft at that time of year. The weeds started growing back so fast that we practically had to begin all over again when the rain stopped. In all, it took us twelve days to finish the weeding. It worked out pretty bad for us, as you can easily figure, and when this farmer asked us if we wanted more weeding work we just told him to go to hell.

Harassed

In Ashcroft on the first weekend in June they have a stampede. These stampedes go on every week in a different town and end with the big Calgary Stampede late in the summer. Indians from all around came to these stampedes. In B.C. at least they have sort of replaced the potlatch-type gatherings. Hundreds of Indians come together for a festive social gathering. In Ashcroft this is when the town officials reinforce the police in order to protect CPR property, arrest drunks and maintain law and order. Two new bun wagons and eight cops were brought down from Kamloops for the occasion. We decided to hand out leaflets telling people what their civil rights were and outlining legitimate police powers — the kind of questions they can ask and that sort of thing. We also instructed people to go to jail rather than pay fines if they were arrested for drinking. Sometimes these fines would be fantastic. It wasn't unusual for a guy to get a $300 or $400 fine or five days in jail; and one guy we know was fined $700 or ten days in jail, for drinking in a public place. A lot of times these people would pay the fine — if they could. I don't know why, except that it was a festive occasion and there was a lot of drinking going on.

Ray, Sid, Sue and I were handing out these leaflets. The police were watching and harassing us — particularly Sue. But every time this cop asked her what she was doing she'd just start reading the leaflet to him. I just walked away and didn't have much trouble with the law. In the afternoon I noticed the police hassling these two old people. One was a very old Chinese fellow and the other an old Indian woman from Highland Valley. Neither of them spoke more than a few words of English, but they'd just sit there and talk in their own languages as if it didn't make any difference. I don't know how they managed to communicate, but every now and then they'd burst out laughing. It was really a funny situation — she'd be speaking Thompson and he Chinese and all of a sudden they'd both laugh. I asked about them and someone told me that they'd been getting together like this for as long as people around could remember. The old man was 108 and she wasn't much younger. He originally came as a slave and then, after slavery was abolished, he started working for the CPR and continued working till he was 98 when they finally pensioned him off.

They were sitting on the CPR loading platform just smiling, communicating in their strange way and watching the fun across the way at the fair. It was the only time these old folks came into town all year. While I was there a cop walked up and ordered them to get off CPR property. The old lady looked angry but mumbled something about not speaking English. Then the cop called her daughter Maggie over to interpret. The old lady just said, "Go hell," and didn't budge an inch. Through Maggie the cop told them he would charge them with trespassing if they didn't get off CPR property. At this the old lady really started laughing, and the Chinese fellow laughed too. I guess they'd been drinking a bit but I don't think it was this that made them laugh. The cop finally got hold of a half-Chinese, half-Indian fellow and told the old man through this guy that he'd go to jail for trespassing if he didn't move on. The old man just burst out laughing louder than ever, probably thinking something like, "Well, it's OK with me if they want to feed me the rest of my life."

Finally, the cops just picked the old folks up and moved them to another spot. They stayed there till the police left, then moved back to their old place on the loading platform.

Later the police told us we couldn't hand out our leaflets anymore because they were causing trouble; people weren't giving them their names when asked and that sort of thing. I just said, "Well, they don't have to." They just walked away, knowing there wasn't much they could legally do to us. But they were furious and even after the stampede they kept saying they were going to get us. "You'll see," they said, "we'll get you for sure."

Somehow we got separated from Ray, and when it started getting dark we decided to go over to Bill's place, not sure if the cops would carry out their threats. When Ray didn't come after an hour or so, we started looking all over for him. Finally Timmy Hewitt, Joey's brother, came over and asked where Ray was. We told him we didn't know and he said, "Well, lets go look for him." So we took off again, this time looking on the Reserve. But we didn't find him and returned to the house. Ray didn't show up that whole night and we were pretty worried. I went back to our cabin to wait, but in the morning headed over to the Thoms again. Then, as I was passing through Cache Creek, I saw Ray coming out of the jailhouse. He was really mad. The cops had picked him up the night before on his way to the Thom's place and taken him to jail for "questioning." They kept him awake all night asking the same stupid questions. He kept asking, "Well, what are you going to charge me with?" "We're not charging you with anything, yet. We have the right to hold you for 24 hours for routine questioning," they said. "Why don't you ask me some questions then?" But they kept keeping him awake with bright lights and questions like, "What's your name? Where do you live? Where do you work?" and so on.

Then in the morning they let him go. He was mad but there was nothing he could do. They did this again a couple of times that summer, just picking him up for questioning and keeping him awake all night. They were trying to harass and intimidate him — trying to get him to leave the area or drop his political agitation.

In late June, just as it was getting really hot, there was a water shortage where we lived. Something went wrong with the ranch well and they had to truck water in from Cache Creek every day. We were rationed in the motel to two buckets of water a day or ten gallons. With this we had to wash, bathe, drink, etc. They said it would only last for a few days, but the thing went on for over two weeks. Our laundry was just piling up so finally we decided to walk into town with it. The Rambler was on the blink; I don't know what was wrong, but it wasn't running.

It was a tough time for us — especially me, as I was getting on in my pregnancy and sometimes a bit sick. I think I almost became dehydrated during the water shortage, and the heat and mosquitoes were terrible. Ray had started drinking pretty heavy again and I was drinking too. In July I got a job as a cleaning woman — or chambermaid, as they call it — for Slumber Lodge, which was owned by Gaglardi, the B.C. Highways Minister. They paid me the minimum wage — $1.25 an hour — and I worked from 8 a.m. to 3 in the afternoon. I walked to and from work every day and it was very hot; the temperature usually got up to 105 in the afternoon shade. I vacuumed, made beds, cleaned toilets and stuff like that. It was disgusting the way some people left their rooms; seemed they would deliberately mess the place up, never picking up after themselves. Sometimes they'd get drunk and puke all over the bathroom. In the morning I'd have to clean it up. I had to finish my work by noon; then I'd do next to nothing for the next three hours. A couple of times I nearly dropped from heat on the road going home. I just couldn't take it, and after a couple of weeks I quit.

After that I started drinking quite a bit; not as much as Ray, but a lot. It was a period when our whole lives seemed to be coming into sharp contradiction. We seemed to be split in two, on the one hand wanting to become more involved in politics and not knowing how to go about it, and on the other hand drinking and slipping into a reserve lifestyle contrary to the kind of political development we said we wanted. We were sliding backwards — drinking, wasting time and becoming politically irresponsible. I realized we were falling into the same bag as other Indians on the Reserve and kept saying we should move to the city. Ray said we should wait; he wanted to continue working until we saved some more money.

One night in early August this crazy white guy from next door came over with a girl and one of his friends — who happened to be the motel owner's son. Joey Hewitt and his girlfriend were over, drinking at our place, but Ray and I were in bed asleep. Well, this guy walks right in, comes into our bedroom drunk as a skunk, and starts yanking our blankets off. "Get out of bed!" he yelled. I was completely naked. Ray jumped up and pulled the blankets back over me, then got his pants on and went into the other room. No sooner had he left when this motel owner's son came into the bedroom. I grabbed a crowbar from under the bed and screamed, "Get out of this room or I'll kill you!"

He walked out and said to his friend, "I think these people want to fight. That squaw in there has a crowbar." I got dressed real fast and went into the front room. The girl was really sloshed and draped all over this one guy mumbling things I couldn't understand. Finally he just threw her out the door. All the time he was trying to get Ray to come outside and fight. Ray just said, "I don't want to fight you. When you're through here why don't you leave."

They were also bugging Joey, taunting him about his size and how he was too little to have a girlfriend. He was only 5 foot 2 inches and about 130 pounds, but he could box and had even won a feather-weight amateur championship. They kept calling him "kid," "half-pint," "punk" and so on. "Come on out and fight, punk!" this one guy kept saying. Joey just said, "No. You're all drunk as hell. Why don't you leave."

Finally, as these guys wouldn't get out, Ray said, "Well, I guess we'll just have to throw you out." I opened the door and the two guys said, "Okay, come outside and fight." But when they were outside, I slammed the door with Joey and Ray still inside. This really made those assholes mad. They started yelling and kicking at the door, finally breaking it open and storming in to attack Ray and Joey. While they were fighting this drunken girl came up to me and wanted to fight too. "Just fuck off!" I said, and went into the bedroom.

Joey really beat up on the guy, but Ray had a worse time with the other one. He ended up getting a broken nose. When it was over, both the white guys left, beaten up pretty bad and swearing at us.

A week later four guys came over — friends of the character next door. This time Ray and I were alone. They harassed us all bloody night, calling us every name in the book and trying to get Ray mad enough so's he'd go out and fight. We reinforced the door and Ray stayed inside. It was almost morning when these jerks left.

That day we went out and bought a gun. Ray said, "If

they bother us again, I'll just blast them." Well, a few nights later, with Dave Hanuse and my little brother Gord up for a visit, these four guys came back. They started shouting again and asking for a fight. We'd all been drinking and it seemed pretty strange. Ray just got up all of a sudden, grabbed his gun and started loading it. "Shoot over their heads," I said. "Don't actually shoot them." Ray said, "If one of 'em comes in here I'm gonna blow his leg off. I'm sick and tired of being harassed by these bastards!" I said, "You're kidding, Ray. You can't just shoot people like that." "You'll see," he replied, "I'm going to blast the first one right in the kneecap!"

Just at that moment these guys walked in. The door hadn't been locked. Ray had finished loading the pistol and raised it, pointing at this guy's leg. He fired a shot just as I hit his arm. Luckily, he missed. The four guys were scared shitless and ran out of the house. I said, "You were really going to shoot him?" "Fucking right! And I will shoot him if he ever comes back — any of them!""But you can't go around shooting people, Ray," I said. "You're an Indian and the cops'll put you away for life!" "I don't care," he said, "I've taken all the shit I'm gonna take from these guys!"

Fortunately, we didn't have any more trouble from these white guys. Guess they were scared off for good. But our lives were still going backwards. We continued drinking a lot — especially Ray — and we were arguing and fighting more than ever. I was getting really sick of it and told Ray I was going back to Vancouver. Ray just said, "You can leave if you want. I'm not sure yet." "You can come when you're ready," I told him.

So in mid-August I left. Ray quit his job the week before, but he was just running around town, drinking and doing nothing. They'd drive around in Joey's car, always getting

Confronting White Chauvinism

I stayed at my mom's and soon got a job as a waitress at the River Queen nightclub. I was working six days a week, ten hour shifts. The place opened up at 10 p.m. and closed at 6 a.m. We had to get there two hours before it opened in order to clean the place, set up the tables, put out the linen and prepare the kitchen. Most clubs hired janitorial staff for this work, paying something like $20 a day for the job. But not the owner of the River Queen; he had his cooks, waitress and even he himself cleaning the place for two hours before opening. It probably ended up costing more this way, paying a whole bunch of people's wages for those two hours. I couldn't figure it out.

The River Queen was really a hangout for weirdos of every variety. The hours were bad, though with the tips and minimum wage I was able to save a little money. I cut down drinking quite a bit, just having a glass of wine before work and a little after I got home. It seemed like I wasn't able to do anything during this period, not even read. I was just sleeping, eating dinner, getting ready for work, working, coming home, unwinding for three or four hours, then going to sleep again. The music at the club was so loud and the atmosphere so hectic that it really took several hours just to wind down after I got home, so I was just existing, not doing much except working, eating and sleeping. I might have quit drinking altogether, but it seemed I needed a shot of wine before and especially after work, just to relax.

Ray came back to Vancouver about two weeks after me. We rented a place in town, near 6th and Main, at the end of August. After four or five weeks of work at the club I started getting these sharp stomach pains. I was also getting thinner and thinner instead of gaining weight, which was the normal thing when you were as far along in pregnancy as I was. So I made an appointment with a doctor in late September. He told me to stay in bed for a few days, until the stomach pains went away. After that I was to take it easy if I didn't want to lose the baby. That meant quitting my job at the River Queen, which I did. In fact, I decided that I'd never work in clubs again. The general atmosphere made me sick, and so did most of the people I had to associate with. I noticed that a lot of waitresses got very callous toward people after they'd been working a while. It was a real buck-hustling kind of job because you depended a lot on tips. I remember one incident in particular where this guy handed me a twenty and said, "Keep the change." He laid it down on the table and this prostitute he was sitting with made a grab for it. I grabbed for it too and just beat her to it. Afterwards I thought about this, seeing myself struggling with this girl for a stinking twenty dollars — which really didn't mean that much to me anyway. It was things like this that made me realize how dehumanizing and alienating this kind of nightclub work really was.

The place we had rented was really pretty small and ratty. There were two rooms but they were across the hall from one another. Joan and Dave Hanuse moved in with us and used the other room. As soon as Ray came back he started looking for a job but he wasn't having much luck. We also started getting involved again with NARP. Gordie and Gerri's personal relations were really breaking down around this time. Gerri was wanting to get out of the marriage real bad. She'd been studying on her own for a while and ever since she began he started harassing her and becoming more conservative and resentful. When she came over to see us — while I was still at the River Queen — we told her we'd involve ourselves with NARP again, but only if Gordie left and it became an all Indian organization. We said we didn't think Indians could seriously discuss things around white leftists, who always seemed to have the "correct" answers and explanations. We didn't have to think at all — just do what they told us.

Ray and I really resented Gordie, or having to deal with any whites in our organization. After telling Gerri we didn't want anything to do with NARP as long as Gordie was there, she said, "Well, why don't we just tell him we want an all Indian group and ask him to leave. If he refuses we can expel him." We said okay and then went to this meeting where Gordie was and, in effect, told him he'd have to leave. He got real angry, saying things like: "Who got you the IBM?" "Look at all the things I've done for this organization!" "Who got you this? Who got you that?" "What will you do now? You know the PWM won't like what you're doing to me." He was really subjective about it, hurt and mad. We explained, saying: "It's not a personal thing, Gordie. We just have to learn to do things on our own. When you're here you're always the first to volunteer. And we let you do it because it's easier. That's the problem — we got to learn to do things ourselves."

So Gordie left, though on a pretty sour note. And it wasn't too many weeks after that he and Gerri split up. They were right on the verge for a long time, not even talking to each other when we'd be in the same car, or even acting civil to one another. Gordie was drinking worse than ever and it seemed to be getting more and more on Gerri's nerves. She had never been a drinker, though before she didn't say much about his drinking. At this time in NARP there were only five of us — Ray and me, Gerri, Dave and Hank. Something called the "Think Indian Project" was being talked about but it hadn't really gotten off the ground. Some theological student from Ontario was trying to get it started.

He'd gotten paid to lay the foundations for it and for some reason had decided to begin in Vancouver. He was pretty lazy and slipshod about organizing it, however, and eventually went back to Ontario after leaving it in the hands of this student Jocelyn Wilson. They started having some meetings as early as August but Ray and I really weren't very interested. I started thinking a lot during this period and, especially after I quit work, I was doing more reading than ever. I had been through Fanon's *Wretched of the Earth* and was reading it again. I also read *Malcolm X Speaks* and Mao's *Military Writings*. I even dipped into Trotsky's *Permanent Revolution* but didn't get very far with it because of the heavy academic style. I just couldn't relate to stuff like that.

Mainly what interested me was the thinking of Fanon — particularly his ideas on Native/settler relations and the connections between colonialism and neo-colonialism. My reading was piecemeal, a little of this, a little of that, and couldn't relate Indian politics to the rather vague understanding I had about imperialism. I guess what was important for me during this period was that I was beginning to think seriously for the first time about politics. It was still very frustrating for me, however. I *felt* that Fanon was right and could follow some of his logic, but there were still so many things I was confused about. And though I'd started thinking and doing some serious reading, I wasn't at all sure I wanted to become a political person. In fact, up till then I hadn't even thought I'd have to make such a decision. Politics up to that point was simply something you could do when things got boring; it certainly hadn't yet become an integral part of my life.

Ray was the one who kept talking about having to decide what to do with his life, whether he should go to school and get a career or make politics the centre of his life. At first it sort of took me by surprise that he was even considering it like that. I was still so ignorant about politics that I never even thought about it like that. I had, however, gotten over my strong anti-intellectual attitude, which I'd had for a very long time. This was mainly due to the influence on me of Gerri and Ray. They could talk with leftists and other people on various subjects and seemed able to disagree intelligently with what a lot of the leftists were saying. They also seemed to have at least some view or perspective on Indian life and politics which I didn't have. I realized that in order to achieve that level I'd have to drop my negative feelings about learning. Just doing some reading was an important step for me. Before, you know, I'd been anti-white, anti-politics, anti-intellectual, anti-Marx, anti-everything. Then after many months of discussion and arguing with Ray (who, unlike me, was the quiet, thoughtful type who got along with everybody), it came out that I was unscientific. Whenever Ray used to say that, it would make me mad, "What does science do for people?" I would ask. For me at the time science had to do with physics, chemistry, and laboratory experiments. I'd say, "Look at this science of yours! It produced the atom bomb and everyone knows how cruel and inhuman that is!"

Once I started reading Mao Tse-tung, a non-white, and found him referring to Marx in a very positive way, I thought that at some point I'd have to read Marx myself to see if it

195

made any sense to me. You see, it took me a very long time to learn that the racism and national chauvinism of white leftists I knew gave them a very distorted view of Marx — actually prevented them from understanding Marx and Lenin, from seeing that capitalism was an international system, that revolutions against capitalism were going on in the Third World, that Marxism was a way of making class analysis and not a bunch of worn-out slogans about the working class. That the revolutionary proletariat of today is mainly in the super-exploited Third World and not in Canada and other rich capitalist countries. Well, obviously I didn't think about it like that then — only that my experience made it impossible for me to think about Canadian or American workers liberating Indians and humanizing the system. It was still a very subjective thing with me ... about honkies, Indians, and personal experience.

I also had difficulty with the arch-traditionalism that was very strong among politically minded Indians — and still is. A lot of Indians were simply against technology. They wanted to go back to the woods, back to nature. And they actually planned to go back into the forests and live in the old way. Being an urban Métis, I guess, made this kind of thinking seem way out. I used to ask traditionalists if they were actually going to go naked, like in the past, because all that technology they were wearing might spoil them. "That won't do," I'd say, "mother earth won't like that at all!" Even Gerri was kind of drifting into this traditionalist stuff. And another girl we knew went way off the deep end. She was one of those who argued that you weren't a "true Indian" if you didn't speak the language. She used to say, "You aren't an Indian, Bobbi." I'd reply with, "So what? What's so bloody good about being an Indian in this lousy country? How is knowing an Indian language going to put clothes on your back or food in your mouth? Provide you with a decent living?"

"It doesn't matter," she would say. "All that matters is being a true Indian, faithful to the old ways." This Cleo was so hung up on traditionalism that when she got pregnant she set up a tent in her apartment to simulate "natural" conditions. She was actually going to have her baby there. But when the time came, her friends talked her into going to the hospital.

I generally put down the traditionalist position in a kind of offhanded and arrogant way. I still tried to relate everything to my own personal experience, and if it didn't relate to me, or make sense in terms of my own experience, then I found it hard to grasp and rejected it. My logic was really crude — if I couldn't see or feel something, then it didn't exist or had no real importance. This was the kind of confusion, subjectivism and scepticism with which I approached NARP and Indian politics in general as well as my new-found interest in reading and learning.

Epilogue

I am sitting in my room mulling over the ancient manuscript from which *Bobbi Lee* was born. My misspent youth, the craziness of internalized racism, my own confusion and the holes rent in my memory had come back at me like cruel bill collectors wanting their pound of flesh. In 1975, at the time *Bobbi Lee: Volume One* was first printed, I was pregnant, with my third child, the only one I wanted before I became pregnant, and had begun the long process of unravelling what it would take to get back to the little girl and the woman that lived inside me but who was paralysed by huge amounts of garbage collected for some twenty-five years. I refused in my heart to write the second volume but had lied to the publishers insisting that I would. The manuscript in my hand found its way to an old box where it lay buried year after year, until my memories came back and I could be sure of who I really was.

We have a saying among our people "If you live right the grandmothers will take care of you," conversely, "if you don't live right they will forsake you and you will sicken and die." At twenty-five, I knew I was becoming ill, but had buried whatever memories I had of the old Indians that helped bring me up, teach me, under a ton of junk mail. Junk mail, billboards of prosperity and tons of my own ambitious wishing for it. Junk mail, thousands of letters, words heaped up one upon the other, sleazily persuading me that the 'good life' was possible, and what was worse, desirable. I had forgotten the years at my mother's house where every little item was carefully tended too. "Recycling! We invented it, remember how we sorted everything out, rags to the rag man, old clothes still worth wearing for giveaway, corn husks, organic garbage to the compost, bottles to the depot and papers to the lonely recycling bins. We rarely ever had a full garbage can for the district to pick up." Mom and I laughed at this just yesterday. She, because her mind had always worked in just that fashion, jarred another wonderfully perfect little memory that I had shunted aside. With the environment, recycling and ecology at the head of everyone's agenda these days my dear old mother is experiencing the wonderful rebirth of validation at last, at least … I picked up *Bobbi Lee* and realized how unreliable a child's memory is. I was a child when this book first hit the press, at least in the sense I was not an adult. Somewhere along the line, I had been bent the wrong way as a child and I stayed bent in the wrong direction until the inability to walk woke me up.

I wrote both T'a'ah and Al Grant completely out of my life. T'a'ah because I didn't want to remember that I knew that from top to bottom this society needs an entire house cleaning and we possess the cleaning gear. Al because I could not face that I loved this little white boy from the first time I met him. He was wise, he was different and we loved each other, despite all the dictums about race relations. We rose above all that. If I had to look at the purity and the enormity of that love I would have broken down and realized that the inside of me was worked up by ancient principles handed down from generation to generation and they could not be ignored. I would have had to face the trappings I wore and account for them.

The inside of me was indigenous, but the outside was covered with a foreign code of conduct, its sensibility and its cold behaviour. I contemplated suicide, but not for long. I was pregnant on purpose, I wanted this child and couldn't bring myself to end a child I had called into being. "We owe them something, we call them into being, so we owe them something." And my mother's musings roll around in my brain as I begin. This epilogue is intended to fill in the missing pieces that came alive in my memory through the long process of unravelling that began in 1975 — the year I realized I was too young to write *Volume Two* with any accuracy. Some of those memories are partially accounted for in *I Am Woman* the rest are inserted here on the final pages I will ever write about Bobbi.

Discover Libraries

Libraries are free in this country for those who know they exist. There was one in every school I went to. However, they were all restricted to age and grade levels. No books outside your level could be taken out. Once I learned to read I wanted to read everything. I had ploughed through mom's "Children's Classics" by the end of fourth grade. I mused over the Encyclopedia, I even marvelled over the strangely written words of a French collection my mother had. In short, I read every book in our house. I didn't know that I could go to the public library and pull out books and return them until seventh grade, so I read and re-read my mother's humble library.

My mother knew about libraries, but after working fourteen to sixteen hours a day no one is inspired to spend the precious half an hour before bed reciting trivia about the world outside with one's children. She never told us such things as that. Instead, she recounted what stories she knew about people that would help us get through life; stories of courage and humanism, stories of sharing and collective thinking, stories of strong-spirited people surmounting great obstacles, stories that taught us about our own philosophy. We needed that more than we needed to know about libraries.

It was one summer when I babysat for this white family in South Vancouver I learned about libraries. Mr Wilson calmly asked me to return the kids books to the library a few blocks away as part of my daily baby-sitting routine. I answered sure without mentioning I didn't really know how to do that. Here's the card he said and gave me the address and directions to get there. All the way there I wondered how he got the card. The librarian processing the books, noticed the light skin of the children and commented, "These aren't your brothers and sisters are they?" "No." A moment of silence passed and I decided if I got up a conversation with her, she'd probably tell me how to get a card. "I am their sitter" Good, small talk, lead it to the central question. "Live-in. I don't have time to make it to my own library." (I didn't even know where 'my own library' was). "Oh, why don't you get a card from here. Just bring a note from the people you are staying with and you can use this library." I panned the place. Hundreds. Hundreds of infinitely interesting lives just sitting on the shelf hoping someone who loves words would take them home. I didn't say that. "Oh sure" nonchalantly containing my excitement at the prospect of reading my summer nights away.

Dickens ... Zola ... Balzac ... Jane Austen. Jane Austen. *Pride And Prejudice*. I thought you must have written it just for me. *Sense and Sensibility* ... another of Jane Austen's perfect children. The one that got me though was one whose title I don't remember and whose author escapes me. The story line goes like this: This young girl just before the turn of the century in England wanted to be a banker. But women are all but barred from banking in England. She overcomes obstacle after obstacle, risks family, friends, husbands, children, everything, in the pursuit of her career. Finally, she is a banker — alone — but a banker. She is no ordinary banker either. What began as a simple 'counting house' system in England was changing to the present multinational financial capitalist banking system that we know today and she was part of the shaping of the destiny of the new system. Right at the top. I wanted to be her. The career girl. I didn't know then that I lacked a very important ingredient to make the climb to the top of any white man's totem pole. Callousness. Nonetheless, I was influenced. *Great Expectations* ... Ah, that's what I had great expectations. I read lots of Pearl S. Buck and the one I liked the least then is my favourite now. *The Good Earth* didn't appeal to me because I was trying to bury the self that felt that way about the earth. I wanted to forget the grasses who had comforted me and the trees who had been my friends when no one else was there for me. I didn't want the good earth, I had great expectations.

The dictionary in the Wilson's kitchen got a lot of use that summer as I waded through as many books as I could. Despite the inspiring tales of success that appealed to part of me, the other side of me, the ancient one being buried, still enjoyed sad tales of injustice that are eventually resolved in favour of the victims. Instead of interpreting these works, I just prayed that the happy ending was universal — at least for me. In the end, I was awfully smug about how much my brain was absorbing. It did not dawn on me then why there were no books about Indians on the shelves outside of the trash dished out by the likes of Louis L'Amour. Instead, the absence of our people's stories on those shelves whispered ugly things to my unconscious. "We are not interesting enough to be there."

I remember reading an odd little book about parapsychology. This little book validated all the things that happened during Indian healing ceremonies. It exhilarated me and unnerved me at the same time. I *knew* these things happened. I even knew who the healers in our area were, The Big House ceremonies were never destroyed by the prohibition laws — just badly wounded. My dilemma was that I needed a book written by a European to validate the reality of indigenous healing practices. The little book jarred loose a story of a lost child in northeastern Alberta Mama had told us about when we were small:

This little girl had been lost for hours during winter. RCMP, neighbours — Native and White — searched for her, all to no avail. Finally, the RCMP and some of the neighbours went to see this one old Native woman from the reserve. She described the location of the girl. "She is under a log in a gulch by so-and-so's farm, she is cold, but still alive." "But we looked there, over and over" came the replies of all the men present. "She's there" was all the old woman said. Outside, they decided not to look for her, sure they had covered every inch of the gulch. Sometime later she was found under the log in the gulch. Her time of death was late in the afternoon a day after the old woman had told them where she was.

This story rolled in my mind that summer — not seriously, it was kind of just there. Mama never doubted the power of our ancient intelligence and she passed on her faith in that other kind of knowledge in this little story; I just wasn't old enough to grab onto its significance.

I read all kinds of books, from Melville's *Moby Dick* to Chekov's collection of short stories and plays. I learned to skim the surface of the words and select the kind of books that suited my sense of life. Most of them were what I later came to know as 'classics,' literature. I picked them because they were filled with the rough and ready poor people like many of my own. Their lives, tragic, courageous and indomitable, characterized the lives of the people in our community, but I didn't think about that I just liked them, that was all.

My furious reading drew to a close when I was about sixteen. A couple of years later, the new Red Power movement revived my love of books and learning in a new way. Reading had a function. In the books written by revolutionary writers, lessons could be learned, society could be both understood and changed. But the change I was after at that time was an ambiguous one: justice for Indigenous people in an integrated Canadian society. Hire Indian people to work in the Department of Indian Affairs (D.I.A.) offices, fill the bureaucracy with our own people. End poverty in our homes. Racism, my deepening awareness of how it worked, needled away at my small sense of justice, but very slowly, almost imperceptibly.

With Child

We awoke one morning shortly after moving to Vancouver from Ashcroft and Ray told me he had dreamt I was pregnant. "It was just a dream wasn't it?" "I don't know," I answered solemnly. One of the guys at work had asked me the same question the night before. I had answered a categorical no at the time, but now I wasn't sure. I didn't want a child. Children chart the course of your life for you and I needed to be the sole master of my destiny. I needed to be a sovereign woman, not someone's mother. The dream of becoming a writer floated back to me. I had done little to realize my dream but I still hung onto it.

There was an old doctor still practising in my neighbourhood. He had no nurse and his office was a general calamity — papers were everywhere, the examination table was covered with them. He ordered blood and urine tests and told me to come back next week. I did. "You are pregnant." I didn't say anything and my face registered less emotion than I should have been feeling. He told me that he was supposed to examine me internally, that he could if I wanted it, but he didn't think it was necessary. I was relieved that this part of the examination would be left undone. It disgusted me then to think of some white man probing the secret insides of me. He felt my abdomen and speculated that I was about three and a half months along — too late for an abortion.

His voice came from far away after that and my voice kind of mechanically answered his questions about health and so forth, while my mind screamed at me: "How the hell could you be three and a half months pregnant without knowing it?" I mentioned I was still bleeding on time each month. He looked at my eyes and told me I was anaemic — iron and vitamins and decent food would fix all that. We talked about it that night and decided to adopt the baby out. When we told Ray's relatives each one of them volunteered to be the adoptive parents. This didn't strike me as odd. Many Native young women who did not feel able to raise children adopted their kids to grandparents or older brothers and sisters, cousins, and so forth. Wayne's remark hit home though, "After all, all the children in our family are mine too." Tough old Wayne uttered the gentlest words I had heard for a long time.

I didn't sleep much for a couple of months after that. In the dark I thought about the baby, what she (I was sure she was a she) would experience in the world we were bringing her into. I thought about her as a six-year-old making that lonely trek to school where other children would mistreat her because this country had poisoned their minds about little Indian babies. I watched her grow up in my mind, knowing me as an aunt — never knowing me as a mother.

I was 19 — coming out of teenagehood. I looked back on turbulent years of my youth. I watched myself do whatever I pleased as though I were the only person in my world. I watched myself make decisions that hurt my family without even thinking about the consequences of my action. Teenagehood is the most self-centred time in a human being's life, necessarily so. If we don't, as youth, turn the world to our own selves we would never be able to develop an independent perspective and the world would stand still for want of change. But I was coming out of that time, beginning to think about others before I acted. This consideration for other people was not an obvious one, it was just kind of peeping its little head out through a maze of unconcern and the little girl inside was hot housing the process — speeding it all up.

I quit working at the clubs. They had lost their lustre for me. The money was good, but the stuff you had to put up with was not. Tip hustling, it came to me, was a microcosm of the whole hustle culture that keeps capitalism alive. "Get something for nothing" is what profit-making is all about. Capitalism is a masterful order in which the poor, the labourers, are reduced to embracing the very culture that keeps them on the bottom.

Think Indian

In the midst of this we met a theology student from Ontario. He wanted to launch a "Think Indian" project — a pre-college program in which Native youth could familiarize themselves with the nature of college, the courses available, and discover ways to study without losing their cultural identity. He had asked NARP to participate in the development of the project. We decided to go with it. Together with Vancouver Community College Native students, NARP and interested individuals we put a project together. We secured funding through the city, hired a co-ordinator and began working up the curriculum. There was a heavy emphasis on the humanities, sociology, anthropology and law, no sciences. A series of seminars given by professors, and or lawyers and invited Native leaders, social workers and so forth were set up. None of the seminar leaders were paid. There were courses during the day for those that lived at the "Think Indian" house and evening courses for those that lived outside. By the time it opened I was very pregnant.

Somehow the conversation one Sunday evening centred on the woman question and abortion. I was stunned to hear my lover say abortion for Indians was bad, "When a people are already dying, abortion is just so much genocide." My little girl gave me a good kick and I decided then and there to keep her. That night when I told him I wanted to keep her, he looked very intently at me and said, "I will never desert you, Lee."

It was the beginning of 1970, my sister at 17 was walking about lugging her new son and I was about to give birth. Youth was on a roll. Young Native people from all parts of the province and the country were coming together, tribalism, the village focus was breaking down. We are all Indians, one people with many cultures. Thinking of all sorts blossomed among us. A ground swell, a tide, everywhere in the country little groups of Red Power youth were springing up. I remember thinking what a miracle the Indian way of being was. All at once, every major city turned out Native youth who were talking about the same kinds of things. Sharpesville [*] came alive for us. Vietnam brought out our poetic best: "Who did you kill brother, did you shoot a people struggling to live their own way? Who did you kill brother?" came the impassioned plea of a Native woman all the way from New Brunswick. We had minds.

We had minds; we could think. All that sounds a bit pathetic now, but then, coming from the survival world of having to constantly work to stay alive, thinking, our recognition of our genius was all so new. Youth everywhere were holding conferences, chiefs were meeting, everyone was talking about our rights; rights we didn't dare to believe existed in the 1950s. By some sort of miracle, we recalled the response of Native people to the early civil rights movement. In our own kitchens, those without television came to our house to watch the news from Birmingham and the young preacher, M. L. King Jr., that led his people to grand and glorious civil disobedience and somehow we all knew that this had everything to do with our own lives. Somehow we were all connected.

We moved about this time and began living in a house with two young white boys and me, Ray, Joan, and Henry. We were constantly arguing with these characters — testing our new thinking. They were part of a group that believed Canada was a colony of America. We were certain that you could not be a colony and a colonizer at the same time. They argued on the basis of Marx and Lenin. I went out and bought Marx's *Capital* and a second had a volume of Lenin's selected writings on Imperialism. In genesis of capital, its

---

*   Sharpesville: Massacre of thousands of South African Blacks who were peacefully protesting pass laws in mid-fifties.

colonial foundations and Lenin's comment on the nature of centralized capital in Canada and the difference between capitalist interdependence and colonial financial strangulation, we found the validation of our own thoughts. Our dilemma was that we still needed some European author to validate our thoughts.

.

Child

Thoughts, when they are crimped in a vice of foreign validation, can never really take root and blossom, but we didn't know that. The political differences between us began to take on a subjective note. The house became a battlefield between the two white guys and ourselves, with the white guys unable to remain united. Ray left for a conference in Campbell River on the morning that Tania was born. I was so ignorant about childbirth — well, no — it was more that I was body unconscious. I had been told about childbirth, heard all the young mothers talk about their experiences but somehow I never connected this to what was going on in my body. I woke up that morning, the bed was wet. I had been an incorrigible bed wetter as a child and thought that my old errant ways were coming back to haunt me. It never occurred to me that my water had broken.

Joan and Hank went with Ray and except for Steve, I was alone. I went to the kitchen and Steve complained that I had not washed out my porridge bowl. By this time my spine felt like it was coming unhinged and the contractions in my abdomen were causing me to sweat. "Fuck off, asshole" was all I said. He jumped up and started barking about how we collectively agreed to clean up after ourselves, ad nauseam. I called Gerri. "What does labour feel like?" and a soft chuckle of recognition came over the line. Ray had left her a cheque so that I could take a cab to the hospital but the bank wasn't open and I had no money. It did not occur to me to ask Steve for it, this was Indian business, not his. Her man friend agreed to take me to the hospital.

The scene grew more comical by the minute and had the contractions not began running one into the other I would have found the time to laugh. Steve started freaking out. "I knew this would happen to me. I know shit about babies and here I am alone and you're about to drop." He was yelling like somehow I had viciously conspired to have this child at the precise moment that we were alone. I was pacing, he was frantic, and my ride was busy having a flat tire. Labour is a different kind of pain. Everything feels like it is being torn apart, your mind loses its ability to focus on anything else. The world takes on an ethereal quality and the people in it assume a kind of ghostly unreality. You see and hear as though you were acutely aware of everything but somehow none of it matters. It is a poetic ceremony of creation.

"Do you think that pacing will make it all happen faster?" Steve's voice had an unusual humble softness to it. "Probably" and I carried on pacing, looking out the window and wondering how come they were taking so long, mind-lessly planning what I would do if I had to have her here at home, alone. "Well, maybe you should lie down or some-thing" again his voice was soft, almost mellow. He was really struggling with his hysteria I mused. Finally forty-five minutes later they showed up. "I'll come with you" Steve said. "Great," I thought, "just what I need an hysterical white man to help me through the ordeal." Tania was born in the days when only the husband by prior written consent could enter the delivery room. I was honestly grateful for that. I was still vain enough not to want anyone to see me grunting, sweating and labouring half naked during the birth process.

I waited in the labour room long enough to hear this woman next to me holler, imagine that babies were born at night, assume I had a long way to go then I fell asleep. I was sure the worst was yet to come and I may as well get a few winks in while it was not so bad. The nurse came in and asked me how far apart they were. "What?" "The pains." "They aren't apart at all." She felt my insides, and placed a buzzer in my hand and scurried out. I nodded out. I woke up to the sound of my own voice bellowing "Nurse!" the buzzer squeezed by my hand and the nurse running in and wheeling me out. She was joined by a slightly panicked doctor, both of them running the gurney down the hall. I was smiling. This wasn't so bad. The constant contractions were gone. Only the push pains and the respite were left. They kept saying "breathe, breathe" while they hustled me along. I didn't know they meant to breath shallowly to stop the labour pains.

The nurse finally figured out I had not been to prenatal classes and started breathing like she wanted me to, while the doctor kept yelling "Breathe." I did. In the delivery room, the anaesthetist tried to give me a spinal. I fought back, the nurse held me down and I bit her. Hard. She slapped me and I cussed her out, so loud that the women on the floor below heard me. I kept saying Jesus Christ like I was surprised you could hurt like this and not pass out. Finally, there was this rush of relaxation, joyous peace and there she was. The most beautiful baby I had ever seen. She was perfect, no marks, no wrinkles, flawlessly even features. I laughed and said thank you over and over to the hospital staff.

I stared at her in disbelief, while my mind started to fill

up with her imagined upbringing. The world began to take on new meaning for me. Depth, longevity and lineage was born inside me and grew alongside the growth of Tania.

Marital Conflict

My husband was raised at home while his brothers attended residential school. The loneliness of growing up an only child for the first seven and a half years of his life prompted him to suggest that we have another, to keep Tania company. I thought that was a pretty good idea. It would save me from having to play with her for hours on end, keeping her entertained. At the hospital, they told me to feed her every four hours. Poor Tania, she cried constantly. She was hungry and her foolish mother dreamed up all kinds of problems except hunger — hadn't those nurses said four hours? Finally, I went to Gerri. "She cries constantly?" I told her. "Well," she said looking at her thinness, "everytime Keith used to cry I fed him first, then if he didn't stop, I would try to figure out what was wrong." She was already three and a half months old and had serious throat infections twice. After that I fed her each time she cried and she seemed to be a little better, but somehow her appetite was not so good. The first year of trouble made her less peaceful then her sister, but she survived.

We took her everywhere with us, bundling her up on a board and leaning her up against the wall wherever we went. She watched the world of adults come and go in her life like every Native baby had for centuries. At meetings, she stayed awake for a little while then slept under the drone of conversation about every conceivable issue facing Native people. We believe a child's memory is both tribal and infant. Babies remember from the moment their brain begins to grow; as teenagers, the sense they have, or lack of sense, is based on those memories. Tania's were special. They were memories of travelling to Fort Lawton, occupying the land, memories of fishing demonstrations and memories of complex analytical discussions about the nature of this country, the political struggle our people were engaged in and the direction we would have to move in to realize emancipation. Her sister joined her sixteen months later. In between time there was the closing of the Think Indian Project and the struggle for Fort Lawton.

The early Red Power Movement had its sad moments and its share of joy and victory. Fort Lawton had all these things. Ft. Lawton is situated outside of Seattle, Washington. The army was giving up the base and according to treaty law, all former military land reverted back to Indian people when the military was through with it. Of course, the state of Washington had no intention of honouring the treaty. Two of the girls from the Bridges family came to Coqualeetza (Sardis, B.C.) to our youth gathering and talked to us about joining with them to reclaim the land. It didn't take much convincing. As I was pregnant, I didn't make it to the first occupation. They had to climb some steep cliffs facing the ocean and I would never have made it. I was frustrated but instructed to do publicity work while everyone was gone.I wrote a leaflet, held a public meeting, raised cash, did radio interviews, issued press releases while they all were having a time of it.

One of our people was stabbed in the neck by one of the other protesters and had to be sneaked home. From the patrol days we knew a sympathetic doctor that treated him without asking questions. Still, no one bore any resentment. It was an odd incident. Most of the protestors were good honest people that wanted the state to recognize the treaty law and return the land.

After Tania was born, I was able to go to the Fort myself. We occupied the road allowance just outside the Fort. Secretly, we planned a raid on the Fort. Bernie Whitebear held a press conference and announced that we were giving up the occupation. Woman wept, to my surprise. We all knew this was bogus, but I guess we had some actors among us that could weep and make it look real. The press ate it up. When he was finished, Bernie yelled, "Indians forever" and we dashed by the lone guard at the gate. We heard the guard, panic stricken, say on the radio phone: "They all just ran in ... Stop them? ... I can't, there's too many." All day the army spent chasing down Indians with jeeps. Grace Thore was there. The woman was at least fifteen years older than me and outweighed me by a hundred or so pounds, but she could move. She eluded the army all the way across the Fort. At the end of the Fort she threw up a flag and sat. It was with great difficulty that the army men managed to get her into the jeep and into a jail cell.

Steve was with us on this trip. He remained outside and looked after Tania for me. We stayed in jail until that night. Gerri, Joyce and I kept getting hauled out and asked who we were and where we were from. We kept telling them Seattle but they didn't believe us. We didn't talk like Americans. That is what struck me. Native Americans, talk just like white Americans. It was more than just the accent, their words, the choice of them was the same. They used the kinds of words that indicated they shared the same attitudes about race, colour, class and women. Their disrespect for women was monumental. I didn't know it then, but the people I had met, outside of the Bridges and Hank Adams, who were just like us, were urban Native people who had never lived on a reserve or any kind of Native community.

In their faces and in their voices was a shallowness and a hardness. I shared the hardness but didn't care to look at it, not then. Intellectually, we could see that racism was bad, but that didn't change the feelings of some of them toward other people of colour. Black jokes, Chinese jokes, and just general bad mouthing about every other kind of "nigger" rolled easily off their tongues. Bernie Whitebear, the Bridges and a woman named Ramona Bennett tried to keep everything together and appealed to good sense and our own ways to curb the negative behaviour but they were a minority. We referred to one group of these guys — most were men — as the 'get-it-on gang.' The American people have a long standing anti-intellectual tradition among its rank and file, despite the fact that some of the best literature was born in the United States. The 'get-it-on gang' shared this attitude, making fun of the Canadians who 'talk smart' and 'use big words'. We were hurt but undaunted; we waged a war of words with them, trying to make them see things differently.

We stayed again outside the camp. We ate communally, virtually out of the same pot. Town Indians let us use their home to shower and we slept in the tents outside at night. Mostly, we just talked and sang. It was good to hear our own music rolling out from the throats of youth. It reminded me of being a child and hearing only the old people sing. No children, just old people. I used to cry inside myself every time I heard our songs. I guess I felt all the beautiful things of the past were dead and gone. At the camp, at night, with army jeeps loaded with machine guns and search lights all trained on us, these songs took on a new life. They represented a kind of hope I had never felt before.

The battle was partially won and Day Break Star was to emerge as a Cultural Centre a few years later, but the concept of the centre was born at the camp, where the possibility of winning sparked the imagination of the occupiers. We were a devoted little crew of campers whose devotion grew alongside the concept of Day Break Star. We weathered over four months of occupation. While most of the men behaved themselves, there was an undercurrent of drug and alcohol use that became evident after a short time. We felt it, some of us women, before any evidence of it showed up. One night, one of the women whose homes people were using was trashed. Some of our own people participated. She didn't lose her enthusiasm for the 'struggle' but she definitely closed the doors to her home.

Youth Implosion

The youth movement of the sixties, blossomed and with its growth a parallel movement of adults developed. The government funded Native organizations seemed to usurp the youth movement, not physically at first, but in invisible kinds of ways. The initiative of the youth dwindled as the organizations gained prominence. The press, hot after stories of the Red Power Youth began devoting its time to reporting the happenings of the Chief's Conferences, Homemaker's conferences, government consultative talks, and other such impotent activities.

When the youth movement began, money was not an issue. With the advent of government funded Native organizations, money became a prime consideration in the organizing process. Many of us objected, but weren't sure why. Some of us were jealous I suppose that they should be getting all that money. The youth movement eventually gave

217

into temptation. We applied for and received some seventy five thousand dollars for a summer's worth of work. By the end of the so-called project we disagreed violently about the reportage that the receipt of the grant required. Some wanted to tell the 'truth', some wanted to tell them what they wanted to hear, others didn't think we ought to say anything to government. It struck me then, that the levels of loyalty to government increased with the extent to which you were funded by them, that this was kind of automatic. We got talking about it and a few of us figured that this tendency to alter your loyalties must be the reason behind funding Native organizations.

Around this time a man named Fred Favel was printing a newspaper called *First Citizen*. In one of the 1972 issues an article about the strategy for stealing human rights was published alongside a 'confidential' document about the government tactics for integrating Natives.

The process of cooptation that the government had put in place was working. We discussed this and began resisting ideologically from within the youth movement. We didn't realize right away that the sense of 'self-sacrifice,' unconcern about respectability, and the willingness to organize without salaries had already been eroded and that was what was behind the desire to apply for government funding in the first place. No one who is paid to organize people wants to do it for nothing. Our resistance was met with a chilly response. In the first place, people had already begun to rationalize their new status "government owes us this, look at what they have stolen from us,"and secondly, there was the cold realization that this contradiction pits Native against Native.

No one disagreed with us, but none was willing to do anything about it. The tactics of the movement were usurped by the growing presence of the government funded organizations. Fewer people came out to the demonstrations organized by Red Power militants. They began to look like fringe fanatics. At the same time, some of the people became more serious about the nature of change in this country. Revolution, a catchword in the sixties, was still something to be aspired to, but first it must be understood. The Native Study Group was born on the heels of the implosion of the Red Power Movement.

We began with Franz Fanon's *Wretched of the Earth*, reading, discussing it together. Some of us were not intellectuals. The words in the books we read came alive for us. They called us to action. Conflict of class nature began to grow within the group but it did not separate us for a long time. Commitment to revolution bounded us together for many years.

Before the sixties, in our parents' youth, there had been laws against our assemblage and our right to struggle for land claims had been banned. Rising prosperity among white Canadians and the New Bill of Rights coupled with inability to access this prosperity broke the silence of youth. We knew the size of every cheque Native and whites got, including the welfare cheques, were different. There was not even a facsimile of equality in the sixties. Most Canadians still believed we enjoyed the right to be 'civilized' but nothing else. We were already cut loose of the umbilical cord of terror we inherited from our imprisoned parents. We talked with each other about things we didn't even know we thought about. History, law, politics, religion ... no subject was left untouched. It was an intellectually exciting time.

We watched the execution of a young Vietnamese boy on television, not with horror, shock or disgust, but with respect as the boy courageously stood, silent, without fear, awaiting his death. "It's a good day to die" was dragged out of ashes as we all believed it. "Come the revolution" prefaced all our remarks. We dreamed of treed streets, beautiful cities in which its citizenry was not alienated, not afraid of one another, but social, interacting within their lovely new homes, for we were convinced we could and would have to reconstruct Vancouver so that she was pollution free, fully treed and not as crowded feeling. Of course, our plan would end single family housing which we thought rather primitive. Apartments were just high density living, big house style, without any of the social interaction that rendered it human.

After Tania was born we moved to a place that ended up being labelled "Pandora House[*]," it was a house learning of a different sort. It was there that my second child was conceived sixteen months after Tania was born. Children have a very powerful sense of the world around them, they know when their primary position is about to be cancelled by the birth of a new child, regardless of age. They hang on to their own helplessness much more tenaciously than is reasonable. If they are older they regress to baby talk, tantrum throwing and so forth. Tania was very small, but she found a way to express her discontent. From the very moment she discovered that I was pregnant she ceased trying to walk and she did not bother trying to talk until communication with her sister was possible. It was not until the day that I had Columpa that she got off her feet and trundled shakily down the side walk calling "mommie" after me. I began to fall in love.

I had wanted to be a writer when I was just a small child living in North Vancouver. At Pandora House I began to realize that dream. We formed a Study Group that was to

[*]   Mentioned in *Slash* by J.C. Armstrong.

220

last six years. We studied Marx, Engels, Lenin, Mao, and other writers, not from the slavish perspective of a great many leftists of the time, but critically. Everything we studied came under the critical scrutiny of a colonized people. I wrote several articles for the *Seize The Time, Liberation News* and of course our own raggedly little newspaper about the right of Native people to self determination and the obstacle that privilege posed for the working class in Canada. Internally, we all struggled with "strategy and tactics" for a North American revolution. We got to know Don Barnett and the members of the Liberation Support Movement (LSM). We decided to join their group. We joined at the lowest level of their highly structured, centralist group.

It wasn't long before this structure, top heavy and undemocratic, began to weigh on the Native members and one by one we left. I really tried to stay. It seemed ridiculous we could all have the same set of political principles and not be able to work together. I didn't realize then but the style of organizing that people choose is also intensely political. Centralism in North America has a great tendency to become autocracy very quickly. LSM was not different. Leaving was not easy but staying was even harder. When Ray left, our marriage broke up and still I stayed. I missed talking to Native people so much. More than missing my husband, I missed our folks. I was not then able to put my finger on it but I knew we were different. Taping and transcribing of *Bobbi Lee* had already begun and I left somewhere in the middle of the process of transcription.

I went back to live with Ray and we moved out of Pandora House, which in the absence of women and politics had became a party house. Soon the original people left behind moved and Pandora House was taken over by a group of 'hippies' as we called long haired white people. We resumed building the Study Group as an activist organization with a definite set of politics. We engaged in anti-imperialist activities and nationalist Native politics grew in the group, as did the demands of my two daughters.

When they were first born, there were more women in the group, but as time went by and the group began focusing more and more on specific politics, the development of revolutionary theory, the women began to fall away. They were not disinterested, rather the majority of the men and myself and the only other woman that hung in there, were not very interested in what they had to contribute. The intelligent people in our minds were men and those that thought like them.

Sexism

The support of women without children for those who had children was gone. The two mothers left were forced to deal with their growing families by themselves. It never occurred to us that the men should have taken up the slack, although one of them did. I remember typing for the group, writing my own stuff, typing for my husband, laying out leaf-lets, newsletters, speaking at demonstrations, organizing activities, feeding hosts of people, and all the while, laundering, shopping, cooking, and cleaning for the family. Occasionally, I worked a regular job or went to school as well as the above.

This image of over work and under recognition haunts me. I had been in contact with the feminist movement off and on over the years, but could not relate to the kind of waste-your-time-circumvention-cum-white-male-logic of its early days. The level of righteousness left over to me by my

Catholic upbringing always led me to reject whatever is wrong and not try to fix it. Children, slowly, imperceptibly began to change this attitude and the image of the woman who was expected to do it all against growing image of sharing the load took on dimension and focus as time went by.

China

I was working for the Native Information Centre and preparing to quit at the same time. I couldn't deal with the contradiction between our desire to serve Native people on the street and the head office's bureaucratic and respectable image requirements. In Vancouver, the party culture had taken root in our community. Gone were the days of old people, children and adults all getting together to sing, dance or just listen to music and stories. I had not missed it until the European style party wrapped itself around us. Get a babysitter, drink and carouse all night long. Go home the next day and pray that they don't say a word because your head feels like it is already housing a train and one more beep might cause it to explode. I participated in it for a short time, until my girls delivered a message. They would flood the house every time we came home drunk, by plugging the sink in the bathroom and turning on the tap. We woke up to a horrific clean up job. I laid off partying after that. I have since learned that a great deal of naughty behaviour in children is in direct retaliation for misbehaviour in adults. Children's sense of justice is based solely on your ability to take care of them, and rightly so.

One of the women where I worked suggested we go to Russia, the two women working with me said they would rather go to China. "Me too," I quipped. She gave us a name of a woman that would help us get there and left. We looked at the name and the phone number and said, "Why not?" I phoned. She explained what we had to do and I told her thanks. "All we have to do is go see the Ambassador in Ottawa with a group proposal." "Right" from one of the women. I phoned. He told me the requirements and after repeating it to the women we agreed to hold a meeting. Much of the work was done by the three women, me and two friends. It took a great deal of correspondence, organizing, studying and planning with the whole group to raise the funds, to meet the Chinese requirements for funding while inside. Working out itinerary long distance by mail from Peking was no mean feat, but after two years we were finally on the plane, heading for Tokyo.

China, despite all the cynicism, was a beautiful country. The people are so much healthier than they are in North America and health is beauty. The Chinese are a vibrant, alive and beautiful people. I was struck that I never saw any fat people in China, plenty of chubby babies, but no fat adults. They don't look spiritually hungry like people here do, even in their dissatisfaction their faces register a kind of long-sighted confidence in humanity. And the streets, clean streets. No drunks lining the poorer areas of town. No raggedly looking Native people bumming quarters in front of liquor stores. No billboards of white women smiling seductively down at you, half dressed, urging you to buy this or that. And, except for Beijing, no white people. It dawned on me in China that white people really did not like us. I knew this in a way before, intellectually and emotionally, but now the spirit of me laid the bare truth out. It was in the faces of hundreds of nameless Chinese people that I saw the absence of twisted crippled spiritual hate, that I realized why it was so hard to look at white people when

I walked down the street in my own country. Their spiritual selves are twisted. I mentioned this to Ray and we argued about 'spirituality.'

We flew from Kwangchow-Beijing, passing over many kinds of environs. Trees lined the high mountains, deserts in some areas, fertile plains, lush tropical climes. China has it all. We wandered about the grasslands of the Gobi desert near the border between Inner and Outer Mongolia, although the Mongolians and the Hans, say there is only one Mongolia. I saw Chinese society all moving with singular purpose but from different places. Some were still not keen on the commune system and were still surviving with the simple 'mutual benefit societies,' others were models full of pride in their progress. I met National Minorities who have a very different story to tell about the wondrous Dalai Lama and his reverence for life. I saw photos of slaves unearthed from tombs of dead Dalai Lama's and met the sole survivor of being buried alive in a pillar of a lama's tomb. In Wuhan, hundreds of small children followed us for several blocks, shy and distant, smiling and stopping when we turned to look at them, but keeping several paces behind and chatting excitedly at these different foreigners. Those children are adults now and have aspirations different from their parents. While the adults dressed plainly, children were clad in brightly coloured clothes and indulged with as many luxury goods as their parents could afford. No long sad faces of children of colour on the backs of buses, despairing about going to school because she would be humiliated by white kids. The children of China looked happy. In their faces, in the cleanliness of their country and in the sprawling beauty of Beijing, I saw my dreams of the future.

I wanted to sacrifice everything for my own homeland. Not just the people, but my homeland itself. For in Canada, the land itself is colonized and exploited mercilessly. She continuously struggles to birth fish in spring to be over harvested in the fall, young trees meet the chain saws cutting edge in too great numbers. Bald mountains stand, lonely sentinels of human destruction in the holy name of profit. I did a lot of weeping as I looked out of the tower near Sun Yat Sen monument at beautiful, treed Kwangchow and the countryside.

Everything in China is different now, I am told, but for me it matters not. It was a dream that China inspired that I came home with. It is my dream and I have no intention of letting it go.

We were warned about suffering cultural shock on entry to China. In fact, the shock of our return was much greater. It was, I admit, pleasant to walk down the street and not run into a European pinched face. Most pleasant. It was lovely to look at the tanned, red-brown skin of peasants, their black hair and energetic smiles. Mongolians look like us and many of them still lived like Dine-Navaho, in hogan-like yurts in the desert.

Joshua Horn once said of China: "Expect the unexpected." For those who saw China as some sort of model, she must be a terrible disappointment. We never did see her that way. It was the way she made us feel that moved us. "It is so good to be somewhere where you are just a human being, where that is a given," said one of the members of our delegation. And we all wept. The recent movement, the sound of shots ringing out, the failure of the democratic revolution, is simple for North Americans. But I have never had much faith in capitalist democracy. All my kin and I have lived under the dubious benefits of this democracy for a hundred years and we are more impoverished and less able to survive than ever. Capitalist democracy requires a few on top and the majority disinherited: "They know not what they are fighting for," in the words of one woman who was in China during the Tien An Men Square incident.

Corruption! Joe Clark and company cry along with hundreds of well meaning ordinary Canadians, as though we were free of such truck. The difference is that the Chinese are trying to deal with it. Here, apathy sluggishness and just 'business as usual' precludes anyone from even changing their occasional voting pattern. North Americans are very good at accusing other countries of atrocities and hiding from its own. The more righteous it gets about other countries the more it hides. Donald Marshall was let go after eleven years in prison for a crime that everyone involved in his conviction knew he did not commit. When Donald sued the state for the loss of his youth, the media wrote: "Indian retaliates" and not "sues for human suffering." It was as though the newspapers assumed we do not suffer while imprisoned unjustly. "Do Indians have feelings?" It is as though we have no loss to reclaim. Everything we do to seek redress for loss of life, time, land, is interpreted by the larger society as 'going too far.' We are constantly reminded in such ways that we don't deserve anything but poverty, neglect and loss of human dignity.

I am still inspired by the Chinese people. They stand up! Reasonably or no, confused or no, they stand up. The consequences, the shots that rang out in Tien An Men Square, the horror that Canadians expressed aside, they stand up. Please. No horror is registered at the armed besiegement of Six Nations Indians, rather it is the Indians who stand up that are horrifying; arrest, threats of shooting, all of this is acceptable as long as it is white people doing it to people of colour. Let China make its own errors, let it own itself at last.

We are not responsible for the life of the Chinese people in China, but we are responsible for the lives of people and the land in Canada. When are we going to eliminate, corruption, exploitation, death and destruction in this country?

Conflict within our delegation, the words of Norman Bethune about the enemy within, and the very Chineseness of China, made me realize how far I got from myself. *Bobbi Lee* was being printed while I was there looking out the window of the Peking International Hotel and I began to think about how I had erased T'a'ah from my heart, left her out of my book, how I had breathed the ideology and aspirations of Europe into my soul. I thought about how the words I uttered were loyal to my own but the emotional meaning, the character of them, was so painfully European. I wept, was comforted by my closer friends and did not mind weeping because the tears were not tears of self pity but raw courage. I knew I could and would begin the long walk back in time, forcing the lost memories back into the forefront of my mind.

Memory

Years, literally years of poetic remembrance, short stories and fanciful flights into my memory were necessary before I could really see the difference between what I was and who I wanted to be. I had picked up the arrogant voice of Europe not as a language but as a way of being. I had hurt so many of our own people: "Someone told me you were a cop, I didn't really believe them, but we were so fragile and you were so raw, that it didn't seem to make any difference. It was painful to be around you and so many of our people just left."

I felt deeply shamed by the pain I had caused my friends,

my family, but most especially my children. I had felt so inept at resisting the dehumanizing process that urbanization in a racist society means for us. My children paid in invisible and visible ways. My beautiful daughters who were so fortunate that I did not spend more time with them, because violence — pugilistic violence — was always there on the surface of my being. I wanted to be that skinny little wharf rat, quiet and soft, yet still hang onto the resistance that was beginning to define me. I had a long row to hoe. China too, had a long row to hoe — infinitely longer in fact. I saw that. I saw how for twenty five years these people had girded up their loins, hauled dirt by hand and wrung food from an unwilling tired land and still was not near the place she wanted to be. A long and impossible march that she and she alone had made. That is the China I saw. The cultural revolution, its failure, pales in relation to the gentle courage, the patience and the determination of the whole people. There are no fat people in China.

The first year home after China was a bad one. I still raged inside. I wanted to control, control, control my little daughters. China had witnessed the conception of another child in me. One I dearly wanted, for all the wrong reasons. Five years old is when your little ones make their first break. The unhappiness and the rage in me, the negative rebellion spilled over into my little girls and we fought. Only they did not stand a chance. Small, they begged me not to hit them when rage overtook my sense of humanity. Little Tania, running around the room holding parts of her frail thin body, begging "Please mommie don't hit me. I'll be good. I'll be good."

It had nothing to do with drunkenness. I was sober and abusive. It had everything to do with racism and self-hate. I thought I hated white people and in fact, I did not love my own. I see this scene over and over again. Me, armed with a wooden spoon and her begging me to love her. I hear her tears in the night's silence softly weeping and asking herself why she can't be good, telling herself to try harder so that her mommie will love her and I die a little inside. Had I not been pregnant I think I would have killed myself. She was six the last time I beat her, but it took another ten years to still my dirty tongue. It was almost too late. Illness crept up on me that year, my twenty-fifth, deep sadness travelled along with it. My marriage sunk into a kind of crazy oblivion and I did nothing to stop it.

I began writing stories about this time to save my sanity. Poetry and the comfort of my diaries — my books of madness I called them — where truth rolled out of my inner self, began to re-shape me. I could not make Ray understand that I did not really want to write, I needed to. In my diary, I faced my womanhood, indigenous womanhood. I faced my inner hate, my anger and the desertion of myself from our way of being. I reclaimed that little innocent child. It took twenty-five years to twist me and only ten to unravel the twist. I still wrote for the demonstrations Native people held, but I began putting my need to write poetry and stories ahead of the political words that our people needed written. I became a woman through my words.

"The girl can work," is what one person said of me in those days, "but its too bad she's so nasty." I began with my children. I focused on being good to them before all else. Whatever anger I had, belonged to the world of adults outside their lives. Old habits die hard and I occasionally failed, wrote some more and tried again. I faced them. I tried to tell them I was not the person they deserved but that I wanted to be. I humbled myself to them and in the end grew to love them in a way all children should be loved —

unconditionally. I have spent a great deal of time undoing the damage of those early years and am not sorry.

We are friends, my daughters and I and my sons. They are the people I love most. We have hauled ass through mountains of my garbage and the garbage this society heaps upon us. We are all intensely loyal and tremendously tenacious because this little wharf rat knew how to work, possessed great courage and could humble herself to children.

Divorce - Remarriage

Ray and I fought over my need to write. I entrenched. Suddenly, the inequity between us, his male privilege and my female drudgery entered the argument. He really believed to be a feminist in North America was to be bourgeois, that somehow to be a sexist was normal and not to be condemned. People will twist words into all kinds of contorted shapes and justify all types of behaviour. No fight would have existed had he said okay I'll share the work around here. I decided to leave one day. With just enough money to pay half the rent on a small apartment and no money for food I walked out the door carrying a garbage bag of my clothes. One garbage bag after ten years of adult life.

I could not afford to take my children with me. My little son was devastated. He would lean on the window of Ray's home each evening I left him and cry like I had never heard him cry before. He stopped one day. In his stopping, a change took place. He was never the same. His dependence on me died. Mothers can be terribly conservative about their children. We want our children to go on feeling the same kind of attachment to us they felt when they were small and helpless. A piece of me wanted him to remain helplessly in love with me, but the other side of me knew that somehow that was all so sick. Sanity prevailed and all I have is the memory of his small and helpless love.

I struggled along as many Canadian women do, single mother, no job, welfare trying to pay for my daughters' braces and old van and my share of the rent. I didn't eat but one free meal a day at the old Indian Centre. I drank mountains of tea and eventually ended up in the hospital.

I had been plagued with this 'problem' from childhood. It started with a little stitch in my side and eventually travelled across my abdomen and up to my lungs until I could neither breath nor speak without convulsing with pain. It took years to figure out it was a simple allergy to regular tea. This allergy was near fatal on an empty stomach. Western medicine was no help, so I went home. I had a couple of lovers before Dennis reentered my life, but when I was in the hospital I had decided not to keep a lover that I wasn't serious about. My life as single mother lasted only six months.

I was at the Vancouver Indian Center the day after deciding to leave my first husband when I ran into Dennis. He stood there outside the executive director's office and my heart jumped, my stomach got those old familiar butterflies. I put on my best performance of nonchalant casualness and sauntered over to the window and asked him for a cigarette. He didn't have any. He looked at me with interest, asked me how I'd been and what I was doing at the Center. I had met Dennis in Prince George years earlier. He had been my one extra-marital affair. In a crowded dance hall I had heard him laugh, a laugh rich with his sense of self, full of faith in his competence as a man. It had caught me off guard to hear a Native man laugh with such abandon and it had attracted me. We spent the weekend together. Over the years, when I felt I was losing my sanity or insecure about my woman-hood, I had sought him out. Here he was again and I really needed to be loved.

"You look like you just lost your best friend."

"I did" as I remembered that my first husband and myself had once been friends and I knew we had lost that too.

"I'll always be your friend." He said it in a voice soft and deep, but without the sort of seductiveness that is so offensive to women when men use women's misery to hit on them. I needed to know I had friends. The weekend after I sought him out. He loved the hurting out of me and I went away again. Dennis had, over the years, come whenever I called. It dawned on me I was using him as a kind of comfort pillow and I had never offered him anything but sweet moment in some hotel room. I had always gone home.

The most difficult thing for women who have had a hard time as children to accept is the full bloom of kind and gentle love from a man who you know would be so good for you. It is not as simple as the addage "she goes looking for assholes, like a masochist." I knew that marriage to Dennis would re-awaken old dead emotions. Tears I never cried. Sadness I never let myself see would come up on me and rape, driving me to celibacy and hard work to forget, would have to be unravelled. My rapist was a white man, but he could have been an Indian. As a child, a young boy leaped at me, tore at my clothes and was stopped by another boy — both were Native. A good man brings back all the horror by contrast. All those nightmares you could not remember, all those memories you could not talk about, or think about because you would have to feel that way again would come back. They were child memories, empty of explanation, devoid of understanding and rich with terror. No mother wants to relive her childhood terror in the face of her children.

In the hospital in 1979, I thought about nothing else. My children need to see me in love. I even thought about the one woman who fell in love with me in a beautiful and romantic way. I knew I would never feel the same about her, but the safety of it, the receipt of love without really having to throw out the trash of memories appealed to me for a moment.

I retreated with my son to the hills around Penticton to work out where I was going. The day before I left some Native man had driven my son and I home from the Center. Outside my house he had undone his pants, grasped my hand and tried to get me to bring him to gratification. I squeezed good and hard and jumped out of the truck. In the hills of Penticton there is power. The scrubby grass, the cactus, the little pines all whispered in my ear. Sound. Earth breathing comforted me. Under starlit skies I decided to have a different go at life. To forge through whatever tragic memories I had, so I could re-claim the beauty in my life.

Back in Vancouver, Dennis was trying to help his brother ascend to the presidency of the United Native Nations. Revive the movement for self-determination was on their agenda. I did what I could and saw a side of Dennis that was even lovelier than the sensuous love he had given me now and then. For every occupation, demonstration, run for freedom, Dennis was the cook. He worked like I had seen only women work. He believed it was all part of our traditions from the past. He believed that all work was just work, not to be exclusive property of one sex or the other and that everyone should do their share. He tended babies, washed dishes, changed diapers, hauled wood and water and built buildings and homes besides the work of organizing we all did. He did it quietly. I remember talking with his former

wife and both our friend. Despite the fact that their union
had not worked out, she said she always appreciated Dennis
because when her son was small she didn't have to do all
the diaper washing and nurturing of their son. Outside of
breast-feeding their child Dennis did everything and she had
worked.

Dennis came over to visit one day in the fall. My sister
and myself and our friends had this practice of trading kids
for the weekend. We would take turns hauling all of our
children to one of our houses and the other three women
would have the weekend off. It kept us sane and free of the
great need to clobber them now and then. Dennis came in to
11 children and myself in the middle of them all. Both the
babies were crying. He took one of them and smiled, "I guess
I'll have to get used to this."

Our courtship was simple. He took me to dinner once
after that. I explained in a great long monologue a whole
bunch of stuff about how I was twenty-nine, a radical, a poet,
a story-writer — not necessarily good at any of those things,
but completely obsessive and devoted to them, that I would
never cook, clean and wash for any man and I was nobody's
good time girl; if he wasn't serious about a permanent
relationship he should leave me alone. All of which he knew.
He just smiled and took my hand. Two weeks later he said
he wanted to be with me and offered to provide the home
and meat we would need for all three children, myself and
his son. It wasn't half of what I really got.

That first year we spent together seems so far away now.
I spent it in a cloud, a cloud of near hysteria. Something like
shock. Not once in my twenty-nine years had I ever relaxed
in the body of me, content with its form, its colour or its
shape. Dennis, in love and oblivious, trotted around with
me, full of pride and joy. He behaved as though he had won

the pride of the Indian Nation, the one woman who, nurtured properly, could shake the world out of its dreamy apathetic racist consciousness. He believed he could nurture me to health and self-realization. It made me afraid. It brought back all those memories of being told I was stupid, ugly, ugly, ugly. I didn't want those memories, but the joy of being the centre of someone's world was intoxicating. I hung onto him full of rising despair.

My daughter objected. Columpa with her niceness, hid her objection, but she never brought Dennis a father's day card or a birthday card or showed him her school work with pride. Tania, spirited and confident did a lot of yelling about how I had said I would never get married again. She wanted me to be with her father. Jaret, Dennis' son, quietly and politely told me he would rather be with Sylvia and Marilyn, Dennis' previous family. It was a general zoo I couldn't deal with. I cried a lot at night wondering why my children didn't want me to be happy or in love — loved. "They aren't supposed to know about things like that. Be happy they don't. They are supposed to busy themselves with the doings of children, you know living for the moment, playing and wanting to be loved." Dennis had said it so softly the words had felt more like wind than words. "Be patient" was what I learned. I also came to realize that step-parents should expect from each other more than the children can give.

I watched Dennis fix scraped knees, cook, and clean for children who didn't want him there. I watched myself comfort a boy who wanted to be with someone else. Love is hard work. One day, Columpa came home with a little drawing she had made, "To Denis" was written on it and tears welled in this man's eyes. A man, to be a man, has to own a woman's heart. To own such a heart he has to do all the things a woman does: work, cook, clean and care without reward.

And Tania, sweet Tania, climbed on his lap one day and whispered she loved him and was afraid he thought she hated him still. He purred in her ear that he loved her too. She and Columpa were the only daughters he would ever have and he felt lucky to have such fine daughters. They talked for a long time and soon all the children were on his lap or at his feet, listening. I sat in the corner penning out *Sid's Worm Story* and the words I had always known lived inside me came out in the context of great love and family. It's how we are.

It has been a long time since I worked overtime organizing a demonstration or trying to build a movement amid the work of rearing children and tending to a man's needs. Routing out all the sadness, the meanness of racism in the midst of building a loving and loyal family has brought me back memories I had thought lost. Memories of old stories, old laws and our ancient sense of humanity have come back. I still see that lonely child crying in a meadow years ago, hoping the earth would open up and swallow her. The little child that was after T'a'ah died. The child whose mother had to work frantically, obsessively without let up so her children could survive. Her love was endless, but her love was hidden behind the great need to work because the world was unkind and uncaring about single mothers. It still is.

In Vancouver, you can see children on the streets at night, raggedy clothes, playing games in places where it is not safe for them to be. Downtown, in front of 7-11 stores. I imagine their mothers, working, working, working, unable to nurture them. I imagine the look of exhaustion their mothers wear. The look of a woman driven to work, as though relaxing a moment would bring about all their deaths and the little girl in the meadow came back to haunt me.

The other day, my other mother, my sister Joyce said to me, "It never was alcohol that destroyed us. It was hard work." The words of Fanon jumped up at me: "Let us stop expecting the Nation in its poverty, in its suffering, in its newly found liberation, to gird up its loins and make greater and greater sacrifices in the interest of the nation. Colonialism stole everything. In any war, the loser pays reparations. Should we win this war, let us demand reparations." The profundity of her remark did not escape me.

It is good to work. But work must be a sane, rational and productive thing. I worked for almost twenty years without pay for a struggle I still cherish. I wrote and wrote without ever receiving a dime. I did so like my mother, driven by the need to be busy, obsessively as though we would all perish the moment we relaxed. In the sunshine of Dennis' love, I learned to relax.

The robbery of our lives has been thorough. It is a complex thing this colonization. On the one hand, nothing good can come of the enemy's money, on the other hand, they stole everything we ever had. Some years back Rolf Knight wrote *Indians At Work*. It dispelled the notions that Indian's don't work. It isn't part of their culture to hold nine to five jobs. I wish our lives had been so simple as nine to five work. I look back over the years and see three girls rising with the spring and summer sun to dig, hoe and weed a garden before they went to school each day, return home to cook, clean and re-work that garden and then, return at dark to their kitchen to do their homework. Year in and year out. I watch my elder brothers hold full time jobs and struggle with school. I watch my mother work. Nine-to-fiving it would have been so much easier.

Rolf left out those institutions called residential schools in which small children tended orchards and farms for the priesthood instead of preparing them for the academic world like other children in this country. He left out the children who left home each summer to work in the berry camps, the sugar beet fields, the ranches and the vegetable farms of this country, because their families could not have survived without them working.

"Indians aren't farmers," I heard one young Native lawyer say one day and I wondered who his parents were. Until the second world war the welfare system destroyed the last of our independent farm, we were farmers, fishermen and ranchers. Many of us still are. Our farms were small, we had no machinery and the land was poor. We got the left-overs of pre-emption to try and force life from. We worked so hard we came to believe that only work was living: "Lazy people should be shot and thrown into the river. If you don't keep busy, the grandmothers will think you want to go home and come calling you and you will die."

No wonder when welfare came into being our parents thought it would give us a break from working till our bodies fell apart. I got so accustomed to work that even while I was ill, I rolled out of bed at six a.m., occasionally falling down the stairs and set to work. Dennis stopped me one day.

"Where are you going in such a hurry." I didn't have an answer. It took five years before I could sleep until I was rested without feeling treacherous or guilty. Still, I watch what financial dependence has done to our families on welfare and the dependence of Native politics on govern-ment goodwill and know self-reliance must guide our eman-cipation. Not the sort of self-reliance I thought we needed yesterday. The sort of self-reliance that drove young mothers, myself included, to sacrifice their children's well-being in the interest of the struggle though.

Our labour has never been appreciated and so it has gone unpaid. We have somehow come to feel we don't deserve to be paid for our work. I myself decried Native people who receive an honest day's pay for their work as 'sell outs.' Never again. Until recently, my writing was an unpaid gift to this country. Never again. Our dancers, our musicians, our healers, our teachers, our farmers are all honourable workers and ought to be paid for their labour. We should not be expected to subsist on welfare and work for nothing. I know plenty of young musicians and poets, traditional and otherwise, who don't mind giving away their work. Dedication will not feed us. We should not have to gird up our loins, near kill ourselves with work, just to survive.

We need to be economically, politically and socially self-reliant so that we can re-affirm who we are and come to the Canadian people whole, but this process should not require we starve our young. The need should shape our political struggle. We need land, we need money to develop this land. We need our share of this country. We do not need to bend our values to achieve this. We do not need to give up our principles, our collective selves for this dream.

We need a country free of racism, but we do not need to struggle with white people on our backs to eradicate it. White people have this need as well. They need to stop our continued robbery, to rectify colonialism in order to de-colonize their lives and feel at home in this land. Racism has de-humanized us all. It once filled me with shame and nearly drove me to death. It separated me from my brothers, my sisters, and my beautiful mother. It keeps white people separated from each other. It keeps white people either feeling sorry for us or using us as a scapegoat for whatever frustrations this society creates in them.

In the process of struggling against racism white people will discover that their own lives have not been filled with joy or freedom. If they don't struggle with racism they will never be able to chart their own path to freedom. Their humanity will always be tainted, imprisoned by the horrific lie that at least my life is not as tragic as those 'others.' So long as the lives of white Canadians are riddled with racism they can never sit at our kitchen tables and reminisce about all the struggles, the trials we have been through together and laugh.

I have bent my back to this plough for some decades now. It is Canada's turn. In my life, look for your complicit silence, look for the inequity between yourself and others. Search out the meaning of colonial robbery and figure out how you are going to undo it all. Don't come to us saying, 'what can we do to help' and expect us not to laugh heartily. You need help. You need each and every white person in this country to commend those lone people of colour sticking their necks out and opposing racism wherever it rears its ugly head. You need to challenge your friends, your family whenever they utter inhuman sentiments about some other race of people.

We, I, we, will take on the struggle for self-determination and in so doing, will lay the foundation, the brick that you can build on in undoing the mess we are all in. But so long as your own home needs cleaning, don't come to mine, broom in hand. Don't wait for me to jump up, put my back to the plough, whenever racism shows itself. You need to get out there and object, all by yourself.

We have worked hard enough for you.

Photo by: Brenda Hemsing

Lee Maracle is the author of *I Am Woman* (Write-On Press, North Vancouver). She has published several articles in magazines, newsletters, and collaborated on numerous poetry-music tapes with other Native and Black poets in Canada. As well, several pieces of non-fiction have been published in anthologies or are slated for publication. She is currently a full-time student at Simon Fraser University and is working on a collection of short stories and two books of poetry. Between all of that Lee travels, reads poetry and tries to keep her children fed and on-track.